The Twelve Steps,
Twelve Traditions, and Twelve Concepts
of Debtors Anonymous

The Twelve Steps, Twelve Traditions, and Twelve Concepts of Debtors Anonymous

෴

Thirty-six Principles
of Recovery

DEBTORS
ANONYMOUS

D.A. World Service
Conference-Approved Literature

DEBTORS
ANONYMOUS

D.A. World Service Conference-Approved Literature

© 2016 Debtors Anonymous General Service Board, Inc.
First Printing 2016
Second Printing 2017

Debtors Anonymous General Service Office
P.O. Box 920888
Needham, MA 02492-0009 USA
781-453-2743
800-421-2383 (USA only)
debtorsanonymous.org

Library of Congress Control Number: 2015920077

ISBN 978-0-9913658-2-1 (paperback)
ISBN 978-0-9913658-3-8 (hardcover)

Printed in the United States of America.

Contents

❧

The Twelve Concepts of Debtors Anonymous

Foreword

❧

In 1976 a small group of men and women brought to the world a simple, highly effective program of recovery for compulsive debtors. Inspired by their founder, a member of Alcoholics Anonymous (A.A.) named John H., the group had spent the previous eight years desperately searching for solutions to their chronic problems with money and debt.

What they learned in those years was that they could apply their long-time experience in A.A. to financial issues. As they applied A.A.'s Twelve Steps to their money problems and used A.A.'s Twelve Traditions to create group unity, their individual financial struggles lessened and a fellowship grew among them. In the process, these founders of Debtors Anonymous made a number of profound discoveries.

First, they saw that a key characteristic among debtors was the illusion or belief that there was not enough in the world for them and there would never be enough. In D.A.'s early literature, the group defined debting, whether compulsive or chronic, as "a disease that manufactures a sense of impoverishment in everything we see and do."

Second, they learned that this malady was primarily spiritual, not financial. Although it manifested in a variety of problems and symptoms, the disease of debting could not be dislodged or overcome through financial tools and actions alone, however responsible or thorough such efforts might be, or even through earning more. They recognized that they were spiritually sick people and that they needed a spiritual solution.

Finally, they discovered that A.A.'s twelve-step, twelve-tradition program of recovery, modified specifically for debting, could provide as many positive results for debtors as it had for alcoholics. For the first time, it was evident that debtors could recover from their world of distress and delusion to become sane, clear-minded, prosperous, and joyous people.

In adapting the Twelve Steps for D.A., our founders first focused on the symptoms of their illness: spending money they didn't have, and being unable to recognize and admit their powerlessness over debting. Then, they focused on the solution: committing to not incurring, under any circumstances, new unsecured debt. They discovered that only when they focused on not debting did the many symptoms of debting, including how they shopped, spent, earned, and viewed life, begin to be healed.

With a successful program in place, the desire for a book-length explanation of D.A.'s Twelve Steps and Twelve Traditions was avidly discussed and debated at annual D.A. World Service Conferences. Since the early 1990s, much effort has gone into trying to create such a book. That book has finally become a reality. It represents the hard work and generosity of World Service Conference committees, the General Service Board, and numerous D.A. members over the years. The result reveals how D.A.'s spiritual principles work individually and collectively, how debtors recover from debting through D.A.'s Steps, how practice of D.A.'s Traditions builds and maintains stable and healthy groups and a strong D.A. Fellowship, and how the D.A. message is carried to other debtors through the Twelve Concepts of World Service.

To every debtor, this book is offered in the spirit of love and service, with the hope that all who suffer from debting and its myriad symptoms can find a new way of seeing the world and their place in it.

The Twelve Steps of Debtors Anonymous

Step One

We admitted we were powerless over debt—
that our lives had become unmanageable.

When we came to Debtors Anonymous, we knew that something was terribly wrong. We might have been deep in debt with unsecured credit or charge cards or perilously behind in our taxes, or we might have been struggling to keep up with our bills. Some of us found D.A. in the midst of eviction, foreclosure, or other legal action. Others of us had bounced checks until the associated fees far outpaced the original check amounts. Some of us were alarmed to see our debts spiral out of control as we indulged in extravagant or even frivolous purchases while bills went unpaid. Some of us were self-employed individuals who found ourselves borrowing just to cover business costs or were business owners who were months behind in our payroll or payroll taxes. There were those among us in D.A. who had never used credit or charge cards but were under a debt burden due to student loans or money owed to doctors, lawyers, friends, and family, or who had very little debt but felt trapped in situations where there was never quite enough money to take care of basic needs.

In all cases, we thought we knew exactly what was wrong:

"I've got to get these credit cards paid off. Then I'll be OK."

"My credit score is shot, I just have to rebuild it."

"If I could only get the tax authorities (or my spouse/partner or my boss or these creditors) off my back, I'd be fine."

"I have to get my phone (or power or Internet) turned back on."

"If I can cut expenses, I'll be able to get by."

"If I could just learn to save money, I wouldn't have to borrow it."

Then there is the one that so many of us saw as a panacea before D.A.:

"I just need to make more money."

It really seemed to us as though the trouble were external rather than within. We believed that *anyone* in our circumstances would have used debt the way we did; it was a bad economy or bad luck or a crisis or a moment of need that was to blame. If we did think we were at fault, we believed that we lacked sufficient discipline or financial experience or mathematical ability. If we could just learn these things, we would handle our money like other people. We declared bankruptcy, convinced that we were entitled to start over after a run of bad luck. Then with a clean slate, we would start fresh. Or we refinanced our homes to wipe out our debt. This time things would be different. However, we who did in fact gain new skills, perhaps even managing to live by a budget or a credit counseling plan for a while, soon found ourselves once again slipping behind and living beyond our means. What, then, is our problem?

Step One tells us the true nature of what we are dealing with, namely, that we are *powerless over debt*. It wasn't that we needed to better understand our debting behavior, figure out a smarter way to manage our money, get control over our spending, learn the rules of smart borrowing, or even earn more money. There are many individuals who can improve their lives by doing these things, but for us, such methods were not sufficient. Unlike most people, we of Debtors Anonymous found ourselves in the grip of a chronic, progressive illness: compulsive debting.

What does it mean to be a compulsive debtor? It means that our behavior with debt is characterized by compulsion—a consuming need to engage in certain behaviors that, although they may provide a sense of triumph or satisfaction or security in the short run, in the end cause pain and unmanageability in our lives and in the lives of those around us. In the midst of our compulsion, we really believe that purchasing a certain item will make us fit in or make us happy. We really think that we must write checks to pay bills whether or not there are sufficient funds in our bank account. We truly believe that, even though we are repeating a behavior that has caused us financial and emotional trouble many times before, somehow this time it will be OK. Or we just close our eyes and spend.

Powerlessness over debt shows up in a variety of patterns. Some of us engaged in compulsive use of credit or charge cards to purchase things even when we had the money to pay for them. Some compulsively borrowed unsecured funds to make ends meet, whether through loans with institutions or personal loans from family or friends. Some of us could not break free of impulse shopping, compulsively using our credit or charge cards to purchase gifts for ourselves or others without a moment's thought to how we would pay for them. Some of us were stuck in situations where we were never properly compensated for our work and were chronically behind in purchasing necessities and paying bills. In some cases, we were living as paupers, refusing to spend what little money we did have because we feared the disaster that would wipe us out. In all cases, our behaviors resulted in acquisition of debt that burdened our lives with worry, grief, and shame.

In Debtors Anonymous we learned that, for us, the foundation of our recovery was to stop incurring unsecured debt one day at a time—no matter what. To some this sounded easy, while to others it sounded utterly impossible. In D.A. we learned that it *was* possible. However, the compulsion to live beyond our means was powerful, and those of us with the disease of compulsive debting had to admit our powerlessness over it in order to begin to recover. The amount we made, had, or owed was irrelevant; what mattered was the compulsion and our inability to overcome it alone.

This last point bore further examination. Many of us came into D.A. in the certainty that if we had more money, we would not have to debt or we would be able to make our debt payments with no difficulty. If we had more money, we would be OK. D.A. experience showed that this seductive belief was simply not true for us. Looking honestly at our own histories, we saw that we had experienced the same kind of financial trouble for much of our lives regardless of our income level. Whether it was that first minimum-wage job or a desirable position in a chosen profession, we behaved the same way with debt, and our debt burden increased with time. In D.A. we saw members who had very lucrative positions or highly profitable businesses who were nonetheless trapped in the cycle of debt. To our surprise, we also saw members with relatively low, sometimes fixed, incomes who were thriving due to D.A. recovery. It was vital that we understood that the problem was the compulsion, not the circumstances. Although a higher income was sometimes needed, more money would not solve all our problems; only recovery from compulsive debting could do that.

Another barrier to our admission of powerlessness was the belief that once we understood the roots of our behaviors with debt, we would no longer be trapped by them. However, even though clarifying where we came from might be interesting and useful, it was not sufficient to alter our compulsive debting. The belief that gaining self-knowledge would solve the problem was simply another expression of trying to gain control over the problem, rather than admitting our powerlessness and lack of control.

As we became more willing to let go of our old beliefs, we began to see past our immediate call for help and our immediate desire for control over our situation. We realized that we were afraid. Our fear fed our denial about how we were living and about the consequences of our behavior. When we finally let go of that denial and faced the truth, it was painful, but it also brought us something we were lacking: hope. Maybe there was another way. Maybe the D.A. program would work for us. Maybe our admission of powerlessness was the first step out of compulsive debting and into recovery and wholeness.

This, then, constitutes powerlessness: driven by compulsive debting, we engage in behaviors that are detrimental to ourselves and others and that grow progressively worse over time. Once we have admitted this difficult truth about ourselves, we have begun our recovery journey.

But what about the rest of Step One: *that our lives had become unmanageable*? For most of us, it was the unmanageability that brought us to Debtors Anonymous—the ever-lengthening list of what was going wrong in our lives. Many of us felt stressed out and hopeless about our situations. Maybe we were avoiding answering the phone out of fear of harassment from creditors. Perhaps we were experiencing the shame of having to face yet one more bounced check. Maybe our utilities were getting cut off or we were facing eviction due to missed payments. Perhaps our personal or business relationships were damaged by our debting.

As we examined the unmanageability in our lives, many of us became aware of deeply ingrained patterns that affected much more than our financial well-being. We realized that debting and its consequences governed how we related to the world in general; our disease manifested in our limiting beliefs, in our lack of trust in ourselves and in life. We were plagued by vagueness and a lack of clarity that created chaos in many areas of our lives. Some of us felt stuck in a pattern of always being behind, never seeming to catch up or get current. We lived in a state of reaction to the events in our lives. At the first sign of a problem, we went for the quick fix, eliminating the possibility of a true solution. In the end, it was fear that was in charge, not us. Our experience suggests that self-centered fear is a key component to our disease.

The reality of powerlessness and unmanageability can be tough to accept. Some of us stubbornly refused to admit there was something wrong with us and clung to the idea that circumstances, other people, institutions, or something else outside ourselves was at fault. We often rebelled at the idea that we had lost control and tried to explain how we were different, the exception that proved the rule. Still others of us responded to Step One with a certain glee; after all, if we were powerless, we were not truly responsible for our actions and their consequences. However, when we sat in D.A. meetings and listened to others' stories, we saw that we were not so different after all. We could identify with many of the stories and situations and knew that we did indeed belong. Looking around in D.A., we saw that others had found recovery by living the principles of the D.A. program. Looking clearly at our own lives and at the experience of those who were healing from compulsive debting, we became willing to do as they did and accept responsibility for our actions.

Over time and with help, we began to experience Step One in a new way. Whether abruptly or gradually, we stopped fighting the reality of powerlessness and of the unmanageability in our lives. It is true: before coming to D.A., we were powerless over debt, unable to break free from the compulsion to live beyond our means. It was also true that this compulsion and its consequences had rendered our lives unmanageable. Once we could admit this, we broke through our denial, giving voice to what, at some level, we already knew. As we grew in this early phase of recovery, we were surprised to find that we could not only make the admission but welcome it. We stopped saying, "I can do this myself." It was a relief to set down the burden of trying to do it all ourselves and repeatedly failing; it was a relief to reclaim all the time, energy, intelligence, and creativity that had gone into our denial. It felt freeing, and indeed, Step One was the beginning of freedom.

Step Two

༺

*Came to believe that a Power greater than
ourselves could restore us to sanity.*

In Step One, we came to accept our powerlessness and the unmanageability of our situation. Once we had truly taken that to heart, we were left in a painful situation. We had admitted that we could not handle the compulsion to debt on our own; that our power was insufficient to the task. Where, then, were we to turn?

Step Two told us to turn to a Power greater than ourselves and that this power *could restore us to sanity*. We found this troubling. Some of us said to ourselves, "I thought I was in a Debtors Anonymous meeting, but now it sounds like a cross between a house of worship and a psychiatric hospital. I am here to stop debting; how can a Higher Power possibly help me?"

It was not unusual for newer members to balk at the word "sanity," at the suggestion that we were not entirely sound of mind before coming into D.A. Our picture of insanity did not match what we saw in our own lives, and we rejected the idea out of hand. Unmanageability is one thing, but insanity? Isn't that just a little melodramatic?

It helped us to remember the role that powerlessness and unmanageability played in our lives: using credit or charge cards as our personal or business cash reserves; accepting services we could not pay for; hiding from our creditors by not answering the phone or not opening our mail; lying to family members, customers, and others about our true financial situations; obsessing about our credit ratings when we shouldn't have been using credit to begin with. There were behaviors that demonstrated the symptoms of our compulsive disease: failing to obtain and understand necessary information when signing binding contracts to take out loans or apply for new credit cards; avoiding paying bills, even when we had money to pay them; and holding onto exploitative or manipulative clients in our businesses. Other symptoms that arose from our debting were physical signs of not taking care of our health, emotional instability, and breakdowns in our relationships. We had to ask ourselves: Did this sound rational?

Some of us, those who had at one time or another managed to live within our means for a while, continued to argue. "You don't understand," we said. "I could control my debting when I really tried. I was capable of smart decisions. I had managed in the past; surely I could do it again." If we were fully honest, however, we had to ask ourselves: If we could so easily control our compulsive debting, why hadn't we? If we could stop on our own, we would have surely done so, given the pain that debting caused in our lives.

Whatever might have been true at one time, we had come to D.A. because our lives were out of control. Our own intelligence had not saved us from our compulsion to incur unsecured debt. Step One made that evident. We had repeated the same cycle, thinking that somehow we would find a way to make debt work for us, and we had failed. Yet on we went, same old thinking, same old behaviors, same old results—in short, same old insanity. This is why we needed help, and in Debtors Anonymous we learned where to get it: from *a Power greater than ourselves.*

The logic of this was clear: if our own power was insufficient to deal with the compulsion to live beyond our means, we needed a greater

Power. However, many of us were guarded or skeptical about this. Members talked about a Power greater than themselves and referred to faith. So, was D.A. a religious organization? What was expected of us in this context? What if we were already committed to a set of religious beliefs, or had left a religion with no desire to return, or had found religion objectionable or just unhelpful with our debting problem? Would D.A. still work for us?

We found that the answers to these questions came in good time. If we were still fairly new to the D.A. Fellowship and the Steps, we needed time to look around and better understand the impact of Step Two. Yes, some D.A. members chose to use words like "God" and most spoke of a "Higher Power" and "faith." This did not make D.A. a religion in any manner whatsoever. The logic of Step Two was simple: What was it we lacked? The power to stop acquiring unsecured debt and to find recovery. What was it we needed? A Power greater than ourselves that could bring sanity to our lives, so that we were no longer driven by a compulsion to debt of our own making.

This Higher Power could take many forms. Once we had attended D.A. meetings for a while, we began to look forward to going and found that we felt relief afterward. Those who had walked the D.A. path ahead of us found a peace that we craved; they inspired us with stories of debts resolved, relationships restored, and visions fulfilled. Even when members were having difficulties, they seemed to address them in a sane, serene fashion, speaking of hope and gratitude. Over time we came to rely on the collective strength and wisdom of the recovery found in our D.A. groups, and what was that but a Power greater than ourselves that could bring sanity back into our lives?

Some of us found that the D.A. Fellowship as a whole made for an appropriate greater Power, while others discovered what they were seeking in the collective wisdom of the Steps, the Tools, and the literature. The more time we spent with the program and its principles, the more we realized that they contained not only knowledge and wisdom, but profound compassion.

Others of us looked outside D.A. for a Power greater than ourselves. What we discovered was that, if we were honest, open-minded, and willing, we found what we were seeking. We might have found it simply in the peace of a favorite outdoor place, or in the joy of watching our children play, or in the love we shared with those closest to us, or in a chance moment of awe at the Universe.

Some of us did choose to use the term God and to associate this greater or Higher Power with our religious beliefs. This, too, was a fine alternative. If we had had positive experiences with God and religious community, we found that it fit nicely with the D.A. concept of a Power greater than ourselves that could restore us to sanity.

Sometimes we questioned why, despite all our prayers for help and healing, relief from our compulsion to debt did not begin until we came to D.A. When we were fully honest with ourselves, we saw that, however earnest our prayers, we were asking God to do all the work while we sat back and continued to debt. D.A. provided a route for a Higher Power to show us that we had work to do! And it started with Step One.

There are those of us who were troubled by the idea of a greater Power even after familiarity with the ideas discussed here. We had had extremely painful experiences with those more powerful than ourselves, and the last thing we wanted to do was put faith in another such being. Some of us in this position are survivors of violence or abusive authority figures. To us, a Power greater than ourselves meant the human beings who had caused us such pain and grief. Our growth in Step Two was slow and sometimes halting. We had to find a new level of trust to experience D.A. as a safe place. In time, by taking a chance and trusting a Power greater than ourselves, we were able to find the same healing from compulsive debting that others had. Our painful experiences had not put this out of our reach.

Among Debtors Anonymous members, there are those of us who carried within ourselves a debt-specific resistance to a Higher Power. Whether or not we were raised with religious beliefs, some of us had concluded that God and money did not mix. Maybe we distinguished between a material and a spiritual realm, placing money in the former and God in the latter. We concluded that we must operate without God's help in material matters. More than one D.A. member has observed, "I thought my Higher Power had better things to do than worry about my debt," or "I was convinced that money was too base for God." Perhaps we thought that no matter how much a Power greater than ourselves had helped us in other areas of our lives, we should just be able to handle debt on our own. If we did look outside ourselves, we might have tried to make an accountant, a tax attorney, a credit counselor, or even a book about debt relief our Higher Power. Surely they had the answers and could solve our debt problem. In the end, we were reminded that the compulsion to live beyond our means is not about money; it is about compulsion. Step Two is a vital part of the spiritual solution that offers us a way out of a life driven by the compulsion to debt.

Back in the 1930s, a friend said to one of the co-founders of Alcoholics Anonymous, "*Why don't you choose your own conception of God?*"[1] This choice made his recovery possible. Making such choices has been at the root of recovery for everyone who finds freedom from unsecured debt and a life of sanity in D.A. Each of us gets to say for ourselves, "This is what my Higher Power does or says or is; these are the characteristics of my God."

It was this idea, more than anything, that opened wide the door for us. This was not the God of one religion or any religion; this Higher Power did not have to be called God, did not have to be called anything. Did we believe there was no supernatural personage as described in many religions?

1 Alcoholics Anonymous World Services, *Alcoholics Anonymous*, 4th ed. (New York: Alcoholics Anonymous World Services, Inc., 2001), 12.

D.A. long-timers assured us that many had successfully worked a program of recovery by choosing a Higher Power that was not a deity. Had we abandoned the religion we had grown up with because we did not believe in a punishing God? There were those in D.A. with the same experience, and they had chosen to believe in a Higher Power that was endlessly compassionate, unfailingly safe, and protective. Did we already believe in a God but feared that God had no time for our compulsion to debt? We heard in the strong voices of those in D.A. recovery that choosing to change their beliefs had brought them sanity and peace.

As we continued our D.A. program and worked Step Two to the best of our ability, we began to experience certain benefits. We were growing in our ability to ask for and to give help, and every time we did, we learned a little more about how much lighter our burdens were when shared. Although we did not yet know the fullness of the peace we saw on the faces of long-time members, we had more moments of mental and emotional serenity than we had known in years. We started to let go of the need for immediate gratification, of the need to have something right now, and chose instead to talk to another D.A. member before taking any action that might affect our recovery; this saved us from decisions driven by our self-will that we might later regret. Why was this happening? Because we were coming to believe in a Power greater than ourselves that could indeed restore us to sanity. For many of us, "coming to believe" proved to be an exhilarating lifetime journey and one of the ongoing spiritual adventures of recovery.

Step Three

*Made a decision to turn our will and our lives over
to the care of God as we understood Him.*

At Step Three, we faced a dilemma. We were told that we could not recover from this overwhelming and potentially deadly malady without a spiritual solution, and that having a spiritual solution meant full reliance on a Power greater than our own. Furthermore, we were told that belief in a Higher Power was not enough to bring about recovery from compulsive debting. The recovery that would come from working all the remaining Steps depended on our ability to surrender our compulsion to our Higher Power here and now. To release the compulsion to live beyond our means and replace it with a daily commitment to recovery, we had to give ourselves over to our Higher Power as fully as we used to surrender our lives to debting. To many of us, this felt like we were being asked to give up our independence, financial and otherwise. However, over time, we came to understand that working Step Three was our first experience of true spiritual independence.

Some of us still wanted to know why this Step was so necessary. We had been attending D.A. meetings, keeping our numbers, and practicing the Tools, and things were changing; we were changing things. Surely we were now stronger, better informed about ourselves, and properly educated about the consequences of debting. Surely our own will was sufficient to the tasks that lay ahead; after all, our own will was generally sufficient in other areas of our lives. Many of us had been taught the value of self-reliance, which must surely be useful here. Why was Step Three being called essential?

When we shared these thoughts in D.A., we heard from some long-time members who had found a quick fix in the Tools and then decided to continue on their own without the Steps or who had simply drifted away from the Fellowship to return later. For most, the slide had happened insidiously over time: paying the occasional bill late, getting a single credit card "just in case," accepting a job without a contract, shopping the sales for items that were not needed and went unused, letting health coverage lapse, taking out a student loan—surely, a sober investment in one's future! Gradually they slipped back into compulsive debting, and they began to try to apply self-will to regain control over their lives with the help of the "tips" they had picked up in D.A. Instead, the debting and the desperation increased; driven by their defects of character, their lives were once more overwhelmed with chaos and unmanageability. They discovered for themselves what so many had learned before them and what our literature tells us: neither self-knowledge nor understanding of recovery will protect us from the compulsion to live beyond our means. The stories of these individuals were examples of how will was insufficient when it came to compulsion, and of how compulsive debting was very persistent.

When we were debting, we were immersed in our disease. Once we found Debtors Anonymous, we realized that we needed to be immersed in the recovery process. This did not mean attending meetings twenty-four hours a day; it meant integrating recovery practices and principles into our daily lives. No recovery principle was more important than Step Three, turning our will and our lives over to the care of a Higher Power of our own understanding, whether that was God, reality, life, or even sanity itself. It was the very core of the spiritual program of Debtors Anonymous.

Our sponsor emphasized this to us, suggesting that Step Three indicated that our Higher Power, however we experienced that power, was loving and would hold our will and our lives with tender care. People's stories persuaded us that that care would be there if we kept reaching out for it and providing it to others. This comforted many of us, as we were still wondering what the implications of this action would be. Was taking the Step giving over our whole selves? What if this Higher Power was one that changed our lives in ways we could not stand? For many of us, it was our sponsor who reminded us that we were choosing to believe in whatever Higher Power we chose. We did not have to believe in a loving God, he or she might say, but why not? Indeed, it was clear that this Higher Power was not going to control us like puppets; if that were true, we would certainly not need to work the remaining Steps.

Step Three begins with the words *made a decision*. This again indicated choice on our part, and indeed, a choice we could remake at any time when we felt the need. However, sometimes we saw this as a way out of committing to Step Three. After all, we were just making the decision; we did not have to implement it yet. We would keep looking at it, examining it, intellectualizing about our Higher Power. We could always act on our decision later, right? Our sponsor warned us that this was shaky ground. We were told that making a decision meant acting on that decision. In the case of Step Three, this meant moving ahead with the remaining Steps. Long experience in D.A. showed that procrastinating about any of the Steps was dangerous, as it delayed our recovery and increased our risk of relapse. It also kept us from receiving the gifts of the program. Step Three was a conscious choice of a new way of living rather than continuing in the insanity of compulsive debting.

How did we go about Step Three? Most of us completed the Step with a sponsor, a member of our pressure relief group, or a close D.A. friend.

We began with willingness. With all the willingness we could muster, we used these or similar words to take this Step:

> *"Higher Power, I stand before you ready to be transformed. I place myself in your hands. Guide me on my recovery path. Remove my compulsive debting, my self-centered fear, and my own self-will. May I shine to others as a beacon of your power. May I choose to remain on your path always."*

D.A. members have experienced a variety of responses to this formal process. Some of us felt very different: introspective or joyful or peaceful. Others of us felt nothing at first, but in the days and weeks to follow, we noticed a lightening of our moods or a sense of serenity. Some felt strange or confused, and it took a while to sort out why. There were no wrong emotional responses to taking Step Three; we felt whatever we felt.

We had entered a new phase of D.A. recovery. We had now truly undertaken a spiritual journey. At this point, we began to notice things we had not seen before, the little miracles of recovery. We had heard people talking about them in meetings—the check that arrived in time to allow a member to continue in school, a breakthrough in sales in a member's business, coincidentally meeting the right person to help with a job hunt. This heartened us, and helped us grow in trusting our D.A. program and our Higher Power.

We could not stop short of Step Three and expect to recover fully; neither could we stop *at* Step Three. Continuing the journey of the remaining Steps would fulfill the commitment that we made by turning our will and our lives over to the care of a Power greater than ourselves. We looked to sponsorship, our D.A. literature, and our Higher Power to guide us as we continued to move forward.

Step Four

❧

*Made a searching and fearless moral
inventory of ourselves.*

Many of us found Step Four intimidating at the outset. There are those among us who have wasted months going around and around with the first three Steps, all in an attempt to avoid the fourth. The more we did this, the more we invited compulsive debting to reassert itself. Avoiding Step Four generally meant that we were absorbed in self-centered fear. It was vital that we move forward.

Still, many of us could not help but wonder: What would we have to look at in ourselves in order to be searching and fearless? What pain and remorse would we have to go through? Sometimes the concept of a moral inventory tripped us up, making us think of people—creditors, friends, family members, employers, religious leaders—who had lectured us on what we were doing wrong and how ashamed we should feel. Did we have to characterize ourselves as immoral in order to do a moral inventory? Was this to be an exercise in judging ourselves in an unforgiving manner?

To address these concerns, we needed to continue to rely on the experience of those who had gone before us, such as our sponsors and other long-time members of Debtors Anonymous. They assured us that Step Four was not an exercise in harsh self-judgment but a process of honest self-appraisal. Yes, some of it would be difficult. We would be shining light in all the corners of our compulsive debting and the emotional imbalance it thrived on, no matter how dark. However, we were told that illuminating truths about ourselves, including the unpleasant ones, was freeing. We could not hide from the truth and remain open to the spiritual process of recovery.

How did we go about taking our inventory? D.A. members have approached this in various ways. We have found that the method is important, but the guiding principles are even more important. These include honesty, thoroughness, humility, a focus on our own shortcomings rather than those of other people, and connection to a Higher Power.

In Debtors Anonymous, we learned a great deal about replacing vagueness with clarity. When we lived in vagueness and self-delusion, we could not see our way out of our compulsive debting. When we became clear and honest with ourselves, we were no longer stuck. This was the kind of honesty about ourselves that was required of us in Step Four, and the necessity for honesty was one of the reasons a sponsor's guidance was so important. When we were taking inventory, it was sometimes tempting to revert to self-justification. Our sponsor could recognize this and help us focus on the task and release the old excuses. The more we practiced being fully honest, the better we got at it; the better we got at it, the greater the growth we experienced in Step Four.

Thoroughness went hand in hand with honesty. We had to acknowledge that being honest "up to a point" was not really being honest. Perhaps we wanted to hide some part of ourselves because of our own shame. These were times when we needed to read the stories in *A Currency of Hope* or listen to long-timers' stories in meetings. In doing so, we heard many examples of harmful behaviors that resulted from compulsive debting. Those who told their stories were neither bragging nor confessing; they were at peace with the past. This gave us hope that we could find the same wholeness. When we let go of our resistance, we were surprised to discover that thoroughness was rewarded with a feeling of release from painful feelings rather than being overwhelmed by them.

Likewise, we could not afford to focus our attention on what wrongs we thought others had done to us. Even though we may have experienced many difficulties resulting from others' actions, focusing on them would compromise our honesty with ourselves and our thoroughness. Blame could be as strong a roadblock as shame. Our sponsor told us firmly that we were taking our own inventories and no one else's. We would get no value in Step Four from judging others, but we would be enriched by the practice of clearly seeing our part in our own difficulties. Often our sponsor suggested that we release blame by asking for our Higher Power's help. We could pray for the willingness to see others as fellow human beings with their own imperfections and challenges, and then turn our attention back to our own recovery.

We found that humility was essential to honest self-examination. Being humble meant we saw ourselves just as we were, without grandiosity or self-deprecation. It was the quality that allowed us to keep things in perspective. Throughout this process, we depended on a Power greater than ourselves for guidance. We kept in mind that in doing a Fourth Step inventory we were beginning to fulfill the commitment we made in Step Three. We were not alone in our self-examination; we had a spiritual source.

This then brought us to the inventory itself. When a business conducts an inventory, it assembles a list of what is in stock. How were we to take stock of ourselves? We relied on the collective wisdom of those committed to recovery in Debtors Anonymous, particularly our sponsor. If a sponsor directed us to read D.A. literature, we did so. If we were instructed to describe our destructive actions and identify the shortcomings that gave rise to them, we did so. If it was suggested that we examine the patterns that kept recurring in our debting histories, we wrote about them. In general, we focused on the present, while making use of our past experiences to illuminate what they said about us and where they had brought us.

Whatever method we used, we probed deeply. What was essential was to become fully aware of the characteristics underlying our debting. We were taking responsibility in a new and perhaps unfamiliar way, acknowledging that we had created our own troubles. Again and again we asked ourselves: Where had we been selfish, dishonest, resentful, fearful, and the like? These constituted "the exact nature of our wrongs."

In time, our work on Step Four was completed. We were not given a specific time frame for finishing up; we and our sponsor could discern when we had been appropriately thorough. Occasionally we worried that we had missed something important, but our sponsor encouraged us to bring our work to a conclusion. Focusing on minor details and attempting to do the perfect inventory were pitfalls; we could get stuck in them. We saw that we needed to move forward, so move forward we did.

Step Five

☙

Admitted to God, to ourselves, and to another human being the exact nature of our wrongs.

Though many of us approached Step Five of Debtors Anonymous with trepidation, it was generally mixed with relief. At last, after much work, we had finished a "searching and fearless moral inventory." Now all that we had been carrying around with us, weighing heavily on our hearts, could be released. We did not have to be alone with it anymore.

For most of us, completing a moral inventory had made us keenly aware of our isolation. As we got sicker and sicker with our compulsive debting, we pulled further and further away from others. Fear and shame demanded that we hide our situations, and ego told us that we could handle matters by ourselves. We were left alone to contemplate the chaos that we had created and that had brought us to D.A. However, each of us now had a Power greater than ourselves and typically a sponsor who had led us through Step Four. The ache of our loneliness had begun to ease, yet we continued to carry the burden of our wrongs and our shortcomings.

From the doorway to Step Five, we began to see the true end to our isolation. The compulsion to live beyond our means thrived on secrecy, so we would stop keeping secrets. No more lies about who we were or what we had done; now we would tell the truth, fully and completely, holding nothing back. We were prepared to share our inventory with a Higher Power, ourselves, and another human being. We only wanted to know how to go about this. How were we to choose the person who would hear our Fifth Step?

Some of us were immediately clear on the right person to ask, while others were more hesitant. It was certainly appropriate for us to be thoughtful in making our choice. Of course, we had to avoid the trap of waiting around for the one and only perfect person. If we were dragging our feet, it was probably due to fear rather than prudence. However, given that sharing our Step Four inventory meant revealing some painful truths and experiences, it was important that we chose someone both compassionate and trustworthy. We wanted someone with an understanding of how serious a matter recovery was and why we were going to such lengths to recover. We wanted someone who would keep all that we shared in complete confidence. We wanted someone who would be forthright yet nonjudgmental. We wanted someone who could be reasonably objective. Those closest to us, such as family members, were unlikely to be impartial, and we could not ease our own burdens by adding to theirs.

Most D.A. members chose to complete this part of Step Five with a sponsor. Our sponsor had completed his or her own Fourth and Fifth Steps and had helped us walk through our inventory. Better than most, a sponsor understood the process of recovery from compulsive debting and the principle of anonymity. By the time we reached Step Five, many of us felt a great deal of trust in our sponsor and saw that he or she would be the natural choice. In addition, familiarity with the issues uncovered in our Fourth Step inventory would enable our sponsor to help us work the remaining seven Steps. However, in some cases we chose a fellow member of Debtors Anonymous who was not our sponsor. Perhaps we felt a bond of trust with such an individual and were reasonably certain that this person would be open to what we had to say and be willing to take the time. In such cases, it was important to be sure that the person selected had already worked the Fifth Step as part of their D.A. recovery.

In some cases, there were others of us who chose to go with someone outside of the Fellowship. As part of our spiritual journey, it might have made sense to some of us to complete this part of Step Five with a member of the clergy, a spiritual counselor, or a psychotherapist. Such a person might already have been familiar with the process of recovery through the Twelve Steps; if not, we briefly explained our purpose and clarified what we were asking of them.

It was not unusual, once we had made arrangements to share our inventory with someone else, to feel anxious about doing it. Perhaps we had come from a religious background that emphasized confession, atonement, or some similar practice, and we did not have good memories of these experiences. Possibly our compulsion to debt led to stealing, cheating on taxes, or embezzling, and we were worried about the legal implications. Maybe we had betrayed others in ways that we found hard to express. These were indeed serious matters, and that was why we were careful in choosing with whom to share them. Once we had done so, we moved forward; we did not let fear sidetrack us now. This was a vital step in the journey from compulsion to freedom.

We sat down with our sponsor or whomever we chose to share with and related all the contents of our Fourth Step inventory. We did it when we could have ample time and privacy. We did not endlessly belabor every point; we were deliberate and did not rush the process. Often, as we described our experiences and our shortcomings, our sponsor would put us at ease by relating examples of similar behaviors. At other times, she or he would probe more closely, sensing that we were holding back information. We have even known sponsors who would begin hearing a Fifth Step by saying, "Start with the three things you were never, ever going to tell anyone." This allowed us to break through our shame and express ourselves fully, knowing that we were being heard by understanding ears and caring hearts. We shared every bit of our inventory.

Once we had finished, we paused. What about the rest of Step Five? What did it mean to admit our shortcomings to God, ourselves, and another human being? In being fully honest with another, we had been fully honest with ourselves. In opening ourselves to another, we had opened ourselves to the God of our understanding.

If this did not ring true for us, we took some time alone. We reviewed everything we had included in our inventory, clearly acknowledging our actions and shortcomings. Some of us found symbolic ways to admit everything to a Power greater than ourselves. Others of us chose a location—a place of worship, a peaceful outdoor spot, a private place at home—where we felt connected to our spiritual source. Our sponsor sometimes provided guidance on this matter. Regardless of the specifics, we found a way to bring the Fifth Step to conclusion.

What was it like for us to complete Step Five? Experience on this is as varied as our membership. Whether we came away feeling reflective, celebratory, or uncertain, we had accepted a difficult task and we had seen it through. In time, many of us found that our experience with the Fifth Step provided us with a new level of openness and commitment to recovery, and we built on that as we continued our Step work.

Step Six

❧

Were entirely ready to have God remove
all these defects of character.

I f there is anything about Step Six in Debtors Anonymous that newer members find confusing, it is the fact that it exists at all. Why a separate Step for becoming ready?

Step Six is an invitation to review our journey thus far and to be clear and deliberate as we continue it. When we compulsively lived beyond our means, we might have raced around, preoccupied with trying to control situations or trying to handle the consequences of our debting by ourselves. Likewise, we might have gone to great lengths to avoid looking at the reality of our lives, hoping that the mess we had caused and the shame behind it would just go away. In the Sixth Step, we neither rushed blindly forward nor retreated into denial. Having admitted our shortcomings in Step Five, we became ready to release them.

At Step Six, we began to surrender our stubbornness, self-pity, and self-centered fear and replace these character defects with willingness. When we combined willingness with the honesty and openness that we began to practice in Step Five, a shift began to occur in us. The D.A. program was fostering each of these qualities in us.

In the context of the Sixth Step, being honest meant acknowledging what was true about ourselves and our lives. It meant facing what was uncomfortable or difficult. Being open-minded required us to look beyond our own limited views. It offered us opportunities to let go of struggling in isolation and to rely instead on the collective wisdom of recovery. Being willing meant we would follow that collective wisdom and embrace what really worked. In compulsive debting, our focus was on giving in to the old patterns that harmed us; in recovery, it was on undertaking positive actions.

In taking the time to be as honest, open-minded, and willing as we could, some of us found that we were hesitant to let go of certain character defects. Sometimes we chose to indulge in selfishness, to feel justified in being dishonest or resentful, or to retreat into fear. We might have believed that we needed these behaviors, that we were too vulnerable without them.

For example, we might have truly believed that too much candor would be damaging to us. Maybe we felt that we had to protect ourselves in close relationships, withholding or lying in order to avoid conflict. We may have believed that our jobs or businesses demanded we portray ourselves in the best possible light, and thus we became good at subtly shifting blame to others. Perhaps we even felt pride at being good judges of when to be honest and when to offer an untruth or hold back a truth.

Regardless of whether it was dishonesty or some other defect that we found hard to release, we could in Step Six become ready to try something new. We had trusted a Power greater than ourselves this far; we could continue to grow in trust. Others in Debtors Anonymous had done so, and we could see that they had found sanity and serenity. The fact that we did not know how to live free of our shortcomings did not mean that we would be worse off without them; in fact, if D.A. experience was any indication, just the opposite would be true.

Once we had reached this point, we were close to completing Step Six. This place we were in—this place of keen consciousness and readiness—was a place of extraordinary spiritual connection. When we realized how thoroughly we had been suppressed, how our spirit had been crushed by the very behaviors that we were sure we could not live without, we could experience a whole new openness to and gratitude for the Higher Power of our understanding. As a result of this process, we would be different, and this was no longer quite so scary. We were walking from the imprisonment of compulsive debting to the freedom of recovery, hand in hand with Debtors Anonymous and a Power greater than ourselves.

Step Seven

~

Humbly asked Him to remove our shortcomings.

One common characteristic among the Twelve Steps is that the completion of each is a milestone. We do not always know it at the time; indeed, sometimes months or even years pass before we see how life-changing a particular Step was. This may be especially true of Step Seven. It is a Step well known to work profound changes in us. Yet it is a subtle Step, growing in us as we continue in our recovery.

One might expect the Seventh Step to be accompanied by dramatic change. However, what made this Step so powerful was that it didn't overwhelm us. It invited us in, letting us know that we needed just one characteristic: humility.

If we had not learned a bit of humility by this point, we were not putting much work into our recovery. All of the Steps taught us some measure of humility. Over and over again, we had to acknowledge that we did not have the answers, that we could not stop debting alone, and that we could easily relapse if we did not do the work of recovery. In Steps Four and Five, we acknowledged that our troubles were of our own making. However, it was here at Step Seven that we became truly conscious of the importance of humility.

We might have been tempted to say that our debting taught us humility, but this was off the mark. When we were compulsively living beyond our means, we were certainly not experiencing humility. We insisted on having things our own way. We were sure that disaster would befall us if we could not have the material goods or experiences we debted to obtain, and we stubbornly clung to our behaviors and what we already possessed. Unable to see past ourselves and our wants, we made unreasonable demands on others. Some of us even demanded that the God of our understanding fulfill all our desires. We learned in Debtors Anonymous that this obsession was very much the opposite of humility.

We also learned in D.A. that humility was not the same as humiliation, something most of us experienced regularly when caught up in our compulsive debting. The two words come from the same root, but their meanings have diverged. Humiliation is identified with shame, remorse, and a negative sense of self-worth. For us, it resulted from having our lives made unmanageable by compulsive debting and its consequences. It made us want to hide the reality of our lives from ourselves and those around us. This did not sound conducive to recovery, and it was not. We could not stay stuck in humiliation and shame if we were to move forward.

What was required for this Step was humility. Words identified with humility include modesty and unpretentiousness, while among its opposites are pride and self-importance. However, many in recovery have found that the best definition of humility is teachability. We let go of having all the answers, of always thinking and sometimes insisting that we were right and others wrong. Defined as teachability, humility is the quality allowing us to listen and learn, to "let go and let God," to see ourselves right-sized. We no longer had to be either horribly self-blaming or arrogantly self-aggrandizing. When we became teachable, we were able to get out of the way and let a Power greater than ourselves work to the fullest. We found that it was essential to cultivate humility in order to continue growing in recovery.

We learned from Step Seven that humility was characterized by the desire to seek and do the will of our Higher Power. Step Seven took the focus off what we *wanted* to do and placed it on what we were *willing* to do. When we were living beyond our means, it was our wants driven by self-centered fear that consumed us. Our fear told us we could not face life, pain, or difficulty without the emotional rush or comfort our debting provided. In Step Seven, we were offered the opportunity to release our fear and embrace humility, and to embrace our Higher Power's will for us.

Did this mean that we no longer experienced fear or pain? Of course not. Life still presented us with scary and painful circumstances. The difference was this: when we grew in humility and asked a Higher Power to remove our shortcomings, we no longer needed to cover and deny our fear and pain with compulsive debting and its attendant miseries. We could instead respond with trust and willingness.

In approaching Step Seven, some of us realized that we still had reservations. We found it hard to imagine letting go of certain behaviors or shortcomings. They had been part of our lives for so long, could we really be OK without them? Again, this was our self-centered fear; again, the antidote was humility and willingness. Where we found ourselves clinging to a shortcoming, we asked for willingness to let it go. If we were truly stuck, our sponsor helped us revisit Step Six and become entirely ready.

Step Seven clearly stated what action to take. In humility, we asked our Higher Power to remove our shortcomings. Perhaps alone, perhaps with a sponsor, we took a quiet moment to become conscious of the God of our understanding and offered a prayer such as this:

"Higher Power, I stand ready to carry your message to others. Remove from me the shortcomings and fears holding me back. Help me be who you would have me be. May I choose to remain on your path always."

When we worked Step Seven in this way, we were placing full trust and faith in a Power greater than ourselves. We were not dictating what should be removed and when; we left that up to the God of our understanding. Perhaps rapidly, but more often gradually, we were given opportunities to grow and change. As this happened, we were more and more able to meet life on its own terms.

For most of us, working Step Seven was followed by many gifts. We entered into a new relationship with our Higher Power. We felt ourselves connected to an abundant source of strength. We had less fear and more peace. We could be honest with and compassionate toward our fellow human beings.

This was a good time to reflect briefly before moving on with our Step work. Having not incurred new debt and having worked the first seven Steps with humility and from the heart, we had come a long way in recovery. Here we might have taken a moment to think about who we were when we first came into the D.A. program. We compared that frightened, angry individual who could not stop debting to the person we had become. There were many contrasts. Now we could talk about these contrasts with our sponsor, having a rueful laugh over our one-time stubbornness, barrel-bottom self-worth, or crushing anxiety. What a difference working the program had made!

Step Eight

໕

*Made a list of all persons we had harmed, and became
willing to make amends to them all.*

When we reached Step Eight, we faced two challenges. First, could
we be unwaveringly honest with ourselves about the harms our
compulsive debting had caused? Second, could we become willing to set
things right with everyone, not just a select few?

Often early in our recovery in Debtors Anonymous, we faced at least
part of the financial amends of Steps Eight and Nine when we were
having our first pressure relief meetings (PRMs), usually before we had
begun taking the Steps in a systematic way. Under the care of our pressure relief groups, we began to identify our debts and our creditors.

Making a list is a simple action, but when taking Step Eight, it was
not necessarily easy. It could be painful to contemplate how we had hurt
others. Our compulsive debting had profoundly affected at least some of
our relationships. Family and friends, employers and coworkers, employees and clients, lenders and businesses, any or all of these may have been
damaged by our actions. We had faced similar challenges in examining
our unmanageability in Step One and taking inventory in Step Four. For
most of us, these experiences meant that we were not as intimidated by

the Eighth Step as we would have been earlier in recovery. We had gained some experience in facing tough truths about ourselves. We were also more practiced at relying on the wisdom of Debtors Anonymous and the strength of a Power greater than our own.

When we did hesitate over Step Eight, it was sometimes due to our fear of making amends. However, this Step is not concerned with *making* amends but with the *need* and the *willingness* to do so. When we got caught up in mental images of how others would respond to us, we were reminded to stay in the present and focus on what was in front of us. As always, we could release our fears to a Higher Power, and then return to the task at hand.

Thoroughness was important. Now we had another opportunity to investigate more deeply our patterns of behavior and our beliefs, especially as they affected other people. As we had already inventoried our wrongs, it was likely we were well aware of many, even most, of the people and institutions that belonged on our lists. Many of us found it enlightening to put our Step Four list of people we resented onto our Step Eight list. We noted each of the people we had harmed. If our compulsive debting had brought material or emotional harm to others, we included them in the list.

Here are some examples of how we harmed others. We were selfish and self-pitying, demanding to be taken care of and requiring that exceptions be made for us. In personal relationships, we might have borrowed money and repaid little or none of it; made promises about repayment or changing our behavior, and then broken our promises; stolen items that we used for ourselves or sold for cash; lived with family or friends while not paying the agreed rent; or expected others to rescue us from imminent financial disaster caused by our debting. In our interactions with institutions perhaps we failed to make timely bill or debt payments, despite having promised to do so; stopped making payments altogether; misrepresented our resources in order to borrow money or obtain credit;

expected or demanded that companies write off our debt and let us off the hook; or avoided creditors by frequently changing our phone numbers and email addresses. By failing to repay student loans, we deprived others (those able to borrow without harming themselves or others) of the educational opportunity we had willfully debted to provide ourselves. If we were business owners or had positions of responsibility in business, we might have failed to pay payroll taxes; made big promises to our clients or employees that we could not follow through on; called up clients in a panic, demanding immediate payment of invoices; used business or expense accounts for personal purchases; or stolen money or goods. These are, of course, just a few examples of actions that might require amends.

It was also important to note what was not included in our Eighth Step lists. Like Step Four, Step Eight focuses on what *we* did, not what we felt had been done to us. If we had skipped out on back rent, we did not blame the landlord who had not repaired a leaky sink. When we borrowed money from a family member and failed to repay it, we did not shrug it off because the individual had somehow hurt us. We did not justify stealing from work to cover our debts by complaining about how underpaid we were.

That brought us to the second part of Step Eight, in which we became willing to make amends to those on the list. Our willingness might be limited by resentment, as in the preceding examples. It might be limited by fear, so that we focused on making amends in the future rather than preparing to make them in the present. Our willingness might have been limited by dishonesty, as when we wished to avoid looking at the pain we had caused others through our compulsive behavior. It might be limited by selfishness, as when we reverted to the notion that we always knew best and things should always go our way. If we were trapped in selfishness, dishonesty, fear, or resentment, we had resources on which we could rely. We could speak about our desire for willingness in meetings, with our sponsor or pressure relief group, and in prayer.

When we got stuck in our lack of willingness to make amends, it did not take long for us to feel the effects. We found it harder to maintain serenity and easier to get into conflict with others in our lives. Often we tried to control people or situations, a strategy that did not work any better now than it had when we were debting or in early recovery. However, we found that we could get unstuck. We could repeat the prayer we learned in Step Seven. We could, and often did, pray for willingness.

In doing so, many of us found that we were learning to forgive. We realized we could forgive ourselves for our past behavior, and we saw that we could find forgiveness for wrongs done to us. Forgiving ourselves did not relieve us of the responsibility for making amends; it opened our hearts and minds to greater willingness. Forgiving others did not mean that their actions were necessarily right or acceptable; it allowed us to treat others as we would like to be treated. The more we focused on our part in the harms we did, the more we were able to let go of the resentment and self-pity that often dominated our relationships. We arrived at forgiveness.

For most of us, it helped a great deal to confer with our D.A. sponsor regularly while working Step Eight. Our sponsor could maintain objectivity when we could not. He or she could help us with the balance between being thorough and getting mired in self-blame. Most of all, our sponsor could keep a sense of humor when we lost ours. This helped us see our way through the process without taking ourselves too seriously.

We gave ourselves time to be fully honest and reflect about our willingness. Exactly how willing were we? Would we go to whatever lengths necessary in our recovery to set things right? Could we find forgiveness for others and ourselves? If our willingness flagged, did we keep asking for it to be given to us? Although it was best not to linger too long at this point, it was also important to be clear that we were ready, for Step Eight opened up whole new possibilities for living a life of love rather than a life of fear.

Step Nine

⤞

*Made direct amends to such people wherever possible, except
when to do so would injure them or others.*

Having made the list of those we had harmed and found the willingness to make amends to them, we readied ourselves for action.
With the guidance of a sponsor and a Power greater than ourselves, we
undertook the process of making amends.

How did we go about it? To begin with, we faced any reservations we
had regarding the importance of making amends. We had to address our
fears of rejection, indifference, or disastrous consequences. We had to
acknowledge the self-centeredness that showed up in blame and shame.
If we held onto our fear and self-centeredness, our amends would not be
genuine or complete, or we would procrastinate and avoid them entirely.

For many of us, it was easy to imagine negative responses to our
amends. What if that family member expressed anger at our past behavior? What if that friend no longer wanted to have anything to do with
us? What if that creditor demanded we immediately pay all the money
we owed? What if that employer took us to court? Likewise, we might
slip into the belief that the other person was the problem, or if we were
the problem, that we did not deserve others' forgiveness.

The common thread was self-centered fear. Like all of the Steps, Step Nine was designed to move us from preoccupation with ourselves to willingness, humility, and service. This was where all of the work we had done would come together; this was where we would come fully into a life lived by recovery principles. If need be, our sponsor was there to remind us that our amends were not about how others responded to us. We had work to do. The outcomes of making amends were often positive, but we had to keep our focus on action, not on outcomes.

Next, we reviewed our Eighth Step lists and decided how we would make amends. Here we benefited greatly from the experience of D.A. members who had already worked Step Nine, particularly our sponsor. They steered us away from blanket apologies and vague promises. It was likely that those on the list had heard these many times when we were compulsively living beyond our means. We were encouraged to be clear and specific about what we planned to say and do. Whether we wrote down our intended amends or simply discussed them, we gave due attention to each opportunity to set things right.

We moved into action. For most of us, our lists included individuals close to us, such as family and intimate friends; those not so close, like acquaintances, colleagues, business partners, clients and so on; and institutions, including credit-card companies, tax authorities, collection agencies, retailers, and others. In addition, the majority of us had included some individuals who were no longer in our lives, whether by death or distance.

Family members and close friends were often those most affected, both financially and emotionally, by the consequences of our compulsion to debt. They were likely to have seen us at our worst, whether in the grip of compulsion or desperately trying to get out of resulting jams. We had caused them fear and frustration as we ran up credit-card balances, ignored bills, and hid from creditors. We had violated their trust when we left them with financial burdens we had promised to pay or when we engaged in manipulative or self-aggrandizing behavior. We had brought about hurt and humiliation as we constantly put our desires first. We had deprived them of resources when we turned to them for support because of compulsive debting. They lived through one broken promise and one meaningless apology after another.

By the time we reached the Ninth Step, those close to us had started to see some light at the end of this grim tunnel. As we abstained from incurring unsecured debt, each action we took along the way—canceling credit cards, spending according to plan, communicating with creditors, practicing humility—made it a little easier for the people around us to believe that we were serious about our D.A. recovery. In other words, by the time we were truly ready to make amends, they were more likely to be ready to hear them.

We found that amends to our family members and friends were often ongoing—that is, they manifested themselves in the behavioral changes that demonstrated our commitment to recovery. But even though these demonstrations of change were essential, they were not a substitute for the direct amends called for by this Step. We found that we had to have a clear and honest conversation with each person who had been affected. Unless an individual was simply unable to understand our meaning (a very young child, for example), our task was clear. We were to acknowledge the specific harms we had done and discuss how we would work to set things right.

There was no reason to belabor the past, but neither could we be too quick or casual in our amends. We found a mutually agreeable time to sit down with the individual and speak our piece. We proceeded as we had discussed with our sponsor, remembering to give the other person ample opportunity to say what he or she needed to say. We remained firm in our intention to rectify the situation if at all possible. We spoke with neither arrogance nor shame, but with honesty and humility. We made realistic commitments rather than vague promises. If we still owed money, we presented or reiterated our plan for repaying it. If we were not yet able to do so, we took full responsibility, confirmed our commitment to not incurring any new debt, and stated our intention to repay our old debt as soon as we could. We did not have to apologize again and again; our willingness and action spoke for themselves.

Again, we had no control over how others would respond. In general, our experience has been positive; nonetheless, sometimes the hurt we caused ran deep and healing took time. There have been times when a family member or close friend pointed out incidents that we had not acknowledged in our amends or expressed mixed feelings about our progress. We found it essential not to become defensive. Whether or not we agreed with the individual was not the point. What mattered was that we demonstrated our recovery by listening respectfully and acknowledging the underlying pain. If a person asked for a specific behavior change, we agreed to bring this up with our sponsor.

Our more casual associates might or might not have been as profoundly affected as were those close to us. Regardless, every individual on the list deserved clear and unambiguous amends, and we did our best with each of them. Occasionally we got highly negative responses. A former friend or coworker might deny our request to meet and talk or might not be willing to hear us out. If this happened, we talked it over with our sponsor, and then turned it over to a Higher Power. Perhaps another opportunity would arise in the future; and if it did, we would again do our best. Either way, we found it helpful to keep these individuals in our prayers or caring thoughts.

It was vital that in no case did we make amends at someone else's expense. There was no place for self-righteousness in our Ninth Step work. If speaking up would cause harm to another, whether it be the person on our list or a third party, then we kept silent. When we were uncertain whether making amends would cause harm, we sought input from our sponsor. We kept our minds and hearts open until the answers became clear. Prayer, meditation, and discussion with other D.A. members were often helpful in this regard.

By the time we reached the Ninth Step, we were typically already in the process of making amends to at least some of the institutions or people we had wronged. In abstaining from incurring new unsecured debt, having pressure relief meetings, developing spending plans, and communicating with creditors, we laid the groundwork. Once we communicated honestly with our creditors and stopped making promises we couldn't keep, we were actively making amends.

There were, however, other reasons for making amends to institutions or people besides owing them money. Some of us stole items from retail stores or workplaces, or from friends or family members; some of us submitted inappropriate or falsified expense reports to our employers, or we obtained jobs or credit by lying about our qualifications or histories and then failed to follow through on the expectations we had created. For some of these harms, there could have been legal as well as monetary consequences. How did we approach those amends?

We could not ignore the words of this Step, which clearly call for "direct amends." We had been told many times that we must be willing to do whatever it takes to recover from this fatal and progressive illness. If fear was the only thing stopping us from acting, it was a signal to talk to our sponsor and call on the God of our understanding for help and move forward with our amends as planned.

At the same time, Step Nine told us to make our direct amends without causing harm to others. Among our members, there were those who faced the possibility of significant legal consequences, including incarceration, as a result of compulsive debting. We had to balance the need for direct amends with the needs of those counting on us for support. We could not justify causing undue hardship to others, such as family members who were financially dependent on us, for the sole purpose of clearing our own consciences. However, we also had to guard against using others as an excuse to avoid making amends. Such matters were addressed individually, including gathering input from those who could be negatively affected as well as guidance from a sponsor and other experienced D.A. members.

In dealing with institutions, we made amends with the same clarity and humility that we had with family, friends, and associates. Because our pressure relief groups had worked with us on our debt-repayment plans, we often turned to them to guide us at this stage. Again, we specified how we would make amends before going into a situation. Our interactions with those who represented the institutions were open and respectful. We owned up to our wrongs. We offered to make reparations; or, if we already were doing so, we confirmed that we would continue fulfilling our commitment. If they had specific concerns or proposals, we heard them out and addressed them. To our surprise, it sometimes turned out that the situations we had found most intimidating were the simplest to handle. For example, some of us have approached tax authorities and discovered that they were very reasonable in their payment expectations.

In making direct amends "wherever possible," we had to face those instances in which direct communication was not possible. Relationships might have been damaged beyond repair, and those involved might have told us long ago never to seek contact with them again. Other individuals might have been out of contact for years or even decades, and we were simply unable to find them. These were cases in which we actively turned the situation over to a Power greater than ourselves. Many D.A. members have told stories of chance meetings with one-time friends that turned into opportunities for making amends. There have also been cases in which such individuals did not even remember the offense, however large it might have loomed in our minds. With experience, we came to trust that, if such amends needed to be made, the opportunity would arise in due time.

Of course, some individuals were lost to us through death. Some of us have felt remorse at being too late to make direct amends to parents, grandparents, one-time employers, and others who were affected by our compulsive debting but were no longer living. We turned as always to a Power greater than ourselves and to the collective wisdom of Debtors Anonymous. Some of us wrote letters or said prayers that acknowledged how we had hurt these individuals and expressed our wish to set things right. Regardless of the method, we approached these concerns with the same willingness and humility that we brought to all of our amends.

In cases where a direct approach was not possible with specific institutions, our pressure relief groups worked with us on alternatives. These often included donations of some kind. If we had cheated or stolen from a business entity that no longer existed, we might do volunteer work for or make monetary contributions to a charity that the business had supported. We did this as cleanly as possible. The time and money we donated were at least equal in value to our illegitimate gains.

Our success in working the Ninth Step was measured not in others' responses, but in how we fulfilled the actions required of us. The outcomes lay with a Higher Power. As we walked this path, we realized with amazement and humble gratitude that our lives were changing in remarkable ways. As we applied ourselves to this work, most of us became conscious that the Promises of the Debtors Anonymous program were unfolding in our lives.

When we compulsively lived beyond our means, we were caught in a downward spiral of debt, powerlessness, and unmanageability. Having stopped debting and having worked the first nine Steps of the Debtors Anonymous program, we found ourselves in an upward spiral. Increasingly, we acted out of acceptance rather than anger, willingness rather than selfishness, honesty rather than deception, humility rather than grandiosity, and faith rather than fear. Step Nine allowed the God of our understanding to guide us in removing the barriers we had placed between ourselves and others. Instead of constantly focusing on ourselves, we were free to act from love and gratitude.

Whether we knew it or not, this was the kind of life we were seeking when we came into D.A. In order to continue to live in this way, we had to continue the work, one day at a time.

Step Ten

๛

Continued to take personal inventory and when
we were wrong promptly admitted it.

When we were compulsively living beyond our means, we kept hoping to "arrive," to get to a place where our troubles were over and we had everything we could possibly want. Our pursuit of this unrealistic wish nearly destroyed us. In recovery in Debtors Anonymous, we live in reality, where we either keep moving forward or drift into relapse. Step Ten is a vital part of remaining free from new debt and living useful and meaningful lives.

It is in the spirit of Step Ten that we continue, on a daily basis, to strive for progress in our recovery and to open ourselves to a Higher Power of our understanding. At the end of each day, we have an opportunity to review and correct our wrongs and to be willing to strive to do better tomorrow. We express gratitude for the blessings we have received and for one more day without debting. We start the day with a renewed commitment to practice tolerance and love for our fellows, to continue to make progress despite our imperfections. Having thoroughly worked the previous Steps, we are no longer carrying the burdens of the past. When we routinely practice the Tenth Step, we avoid picking up new burdens in the present.

Many of us find that a daily inventory provides an excellent structure for working this Step. The daily inventory has been compared to a balance sheet on which we list our assets and liabilities as they showed up during the day. How appropriate this image is for recovering compulsive debtors! What were our inflows and outflows, and were they loving or harmful to those around us? We ask ourselves, "Where were we greedy, selfish, dishonest, resentful, or fearful?" We focus on our own actions and honestly acknowledge where we fell short. We ask a Power greater than ourselves to remove our shortcomings and guide our recovery. We also take grateful note of our positive actions.

If the daily inventory turns up a need for making amends, we promptly make them. We set things right as we go. The discomfort of owning up to our wrongs is of little concern when we remember the agony and chaos of our debting days. If we are particularly anxious about making amends to a specific individual, we can contact a sponsor or other D.A. member before and after undertaking the amends.

Our purpose in reviewing the day is neither to congratulate ourselves nor to wallow in guilt. Being rigorously honest, we discover, is its own reward; our lives are enriched, one day at a time. When we fail, we slip into isolation, self-justification, and blame. Less focused on ourselves, we are more open to our Higher Power. We avoid placing ourselves at risk of relapse, with all the misery it brings to others and ourselves. None of us can afford to rest on our laurels. If we notice ourselves doing so, we recommit to taking inventory daily and, when indicated, to making amends.

The daily inventory is also an opportunity to review our use of the D.A. Tools and to help ensure that we are attending to our recovery and avoiding complacency. Though we use some Tools every day and some less often, we need to practice all of them over time as part of maintaining our recovery from compulsive debting.

The daily balance sheet is not the only format for continuing to take personal inventory. Anytime we find ourselves driven by the emotional booby traps of anger, resentment, fear, greed, or a grasping ego, we can pause, step back, and think, assessing what is going on with us and where we are at fault. We notice our thoughts, feelings, and actions; and we acknowledge our part in creating the disturbance. We ask ourselves if we are treating others the way we would want others to treat us. No matter who we think is at fault, we recognize that all people are human, others as well as ourselves, and we move forward in the spirit of developing compassion and love for others. We have learned that pain comes before serenity and that we no longer have to run from pain; we can face it and make things right. We take a moment to share our thoughts with a sponsor or another recovering debtor, and we turn the day's inventory over to the God of our understanding. It amazes us, at times, how much better we feel after a brief phone call and a moment of prayer or meditation. We can then clear the air by making amends, and move ahead with the day, perhaps turning to an act of service to restore perspective.

There are times when larger issues arise in our lives, often bringing anxiety, hurt, or confusion, and we learn a great deal by taking an inventory specific to such issues. Our inventory might examine a personal relationship, a business relationship, our livelihood, or an emotionally charged concern from the past that was not fully resolved in Steps Four through Nine. By now we know that writing is a very practical tool, and we can use it to describe the issue and our part in it. The ongoing support of a sponsor helps us employ Step Ten in this way. When the issue specifically involves our spending, debt repayment, or employment or business, the support of the pressure relief group can be invaluable. We might also seek input from other experienced D.A. members who have faced similar circumstances. Wherever it takes us, this in-depth inventory on a specific issue can go a long way toward preventing vagueness and relapse.

When we were still debting, our financial well-being in the present was held hostage by our past actions. When we stopped incurring new unsecured debt and began practicing the Steps, we were liberated from this situation and could live abundantly in the present with a new spiritual understanding of what freedom could be. By taking personal inventory and making ongoing amends, we experience the same liberation in emotional and spiritual terms. Step Ten makes it possible for us to be fully alive in the present. We then have that much more experience, strength, and hope to share with other compulsive debtors.

Step Eleven

⚘

*Sought through prayer and meditation to improve our
conscious contact with God as we understood Him, praying only for
knowledge of His will for us and the power to carry that out.*

The Twelve Steps of Debtors Anonymous present a spiritual solution
to the problem of compulsive debting. In Step Eleven, we deliber-
ately and directly expand our spiritual lives by cultivating conscious contact with a Power greater than ourselves. Although we might have had
some kind of consciousness of a Higher Power before taking the Steps
in D.A., our resistance to applying spiritual principles to our debting
and our finances blocked us from full and total surrender. Once we had
taken Step Three in D.A., in which we made a decision to turn our will
and our lives over to the care of the God of our understanding, each suc-
cessive D.A. Step was accomplished while relying on our Higher Power's
strength and guidance. Now we are ready to enlarge our spiritual lives as
recovering compulsive debtors through prayer and meditation.

The newcomer might ask, what exactly *are* prayer and meditation?
And how do they keep me from compulsive debting? It is common
among D.A. members to describe prayer as *talking to God* while describ-
ing meditation as *listening for God*. Engaging in prayer and meditation

brings significant rewards, although not necessarily those we might expect. Prayer and meditation strengthen our ability to live life on its own terms, and to meet difficult circumstances with serenity, humility, and responsible action. If we can do that, then we are less likely to act fearfully out of self-will.

Some of us have fully formed ideas of what prayer is, while for others it remains more nebulous. It is not important that our understanding be thorough, only that we are able to open ourselves to it. Some of us already have experience with prayer from other Twelve Step fellowships or spiritual or religious practices. Others never prayed before encountering the Steps of D.A. Some of us value formal prayers—perhaps familiar ones that we learned when growing up or those we have been introduced to in D.A. recovery, such as the Serenity Prayer or the Third and Seventh Step prayers found in this volume. For others of us, prayer is simply speaking silently or aloud to a Higher Power. We put words to whatever matters to us in the moment. Such a practice is often a helpful starting point for those of us new to prayer; it gives us a chance to explore what works best for us.

Some D.A. members have expressed doubt about the value of prayer. In the past, we might have prayed for the fulfillment of certain hopes or wishes and were disappointed when they were not forthcoming. Our disappointment might have been momentary, but at times it was connected to something vital in our lives. We may have recognized the insanity of our compulsive debting and prayed to be relieved of it, only to find ourselves debting again. We may have pleaded that we get out of some financial mess or other, only to acquire yet another round of threatening calls from creditors, bounced-check charges, eviction notices, or demands from tax authorities.

In D.A., as this Step suggests, we find a new understanding of the kind of prayer that makes requests of the God of our understanding. Step Eleven incorporates a specific suggestion: that we pray only to know our Higher Power's will for us and for the strength needed to carry it out. Instead of telling a Higher Power what we need, want, and should have, instead of insisting that the consequences of our actions evaporate, we humbly seek to know what right actions to engage in—what God's will is for us today—and we leave the outcomes alone. This is a kind of prayer that brings closeness rather than distance, connection rather than isolation.

Many of us have incorporated a number of elements into our prayers. Prayers of gratitude lighten our hearts and remind us of all that is good in our lives. Grateful prayer is an opportunity to acknowledge the abundance we now experience, whatever form it may take. Prayers of commitment to recovery, such as asking for help in remaining free of incurring new unsecured debt, remind us that we must continue seeking support if we are to continue recovering. Prayers for others strengthen our humility and compassion by reminding us to look beyond ourselves. For example, when we are in conflict with someone, we can pray for a resolution that meets everyone's needs rather than focusing on what we think should happen. If we are holding a resentment against another, we can pray for that individual's health, prosperity, and happiness. In the spirit of Step Eleven, we practice following our requests with "may I do your will, not mine, always" or some other reminder that keeps our perspective right-sized. However, D.A. experience shows us there is no single correct way to pray; what really matters is cultivating the connection to what is greater than ourselves.

In its simplest and most profound form, meditation is stillness of mind and spirit that allows us to be conscious of our Higher Power's wisdom. Practicing meditation means setting aside other considerations for the moment and opening ourselves to this consciousness. As with prayer, D.A. members bring a wide variety of experience with meditation. There are those of us who have never engaged in meditation, those who have learned one or more formal approaches, and those whose meditation style has arisen organically without training. In D.A., we find that the value of meditation has to do with openness to a Power greater than ourselves. The specific practices are entirely a matter of what fits each of us. Some of us prefer to meditate alone, while others benefit from participating in group meditation. Some use the guidance of a leader or a recording to take us through our meditation, while others prefer to meditate in silence. We find we can meditate while sitting still, walking, or running; in the morning, in the middle of the day, or in the evening; when peaceful, when grieving, or when joyous. For many, meditation becomes simply a matter of mindfulness, of being in each moment as fully and consciously as we can. In short, we find approaches to meditation to be wonderfully flexible. Each of us can find ways to integrate meditation into our daily lives. It really is that simple.

However, as is often noted in recovery, simple is not the same as easy. Some of us find achieving stillness very challenging; our thoughts and feelings wander or jump about, providing many distractions. When we become frustrated, our sponsor may remind us that all of our recovery efforts take time and practice. Like other D.A. practices, such as recording our numbers, following a spending plan, and taking a routine inventory, both meditation and prayer become easier and more natural with practice. By giving ourselves time and refraining from self-criticism, we find the methods that work for us. Likewise, some of us encounter periods during which meditation or prayer becomes more difficult for a time. Again, being patient and trusting the wisdom of D.A. helps us find new openings to stillness and conscious contact.

Cultivating conscious contact through prayer and meditation is a way of maturing in the D.A. recovery process. We grow in letting go of the illusion of control. We find ourselves able to tolerate and at times even embrace things that confounded us when we were debting: experiencing discomfort and uncertainty; having to wait; having to take a frightening, "humiliating," but necessary action. We come to know that our source has never been our job or business, or our parents or spouse, but has always been our Higher Power. We accept that we will always be making progress rather than achieving perfection. In time, many of us find that even not debting is no longer a struggle; instead, it has simply become part of who we are, a daily practice of mindfulness. We truly and humbly appreciate the abundance in our lives wherever we find it. We are, at last, truly alive and free!

Step Twelve

❧

Having had a spiritual awakening as the result of these steps,
we tried to carry this message to compulsive debtors, and
to practice these principles in all our affairs.

When we reached Step Twelve, we found it informative to look back on who we were and what we had been relying on when we started in Debtors Anonymous. Compulsive debting, financial and emotional chaos, and desperation had driven us to seek help; we wanted a way out. In those days, we thought in terms of quick fixes, something to take away the consequences of our actions and all the fear and pain that came with them. We also assumed that what we lacked was self-discipline. We thought we were weak, bad, or permanently defective. We thought that D.A. would teach us how to live by a strict budget, putting our creditors first and denying ourselves what we wanted or even what we needed. Many of us came to D.A. for financial advice; we did not expect to find a spiritual solution for our debting and for all the troubles that came with it. Although D.A. did provide temporary relief through its practical Tools and loving fellowship, what made it possible for us to attain and maintain true and lasting recovery was walking the spiritual path of the Twelve Steps.

There is a remarkable contrast between who we were as newcomers and who we have become through working the first eleven Steps. We lived in fear of scarcity and deprivation as a result of our debting; now we have a new view of, and gratitude for, our own prosperity and abundance. We thought that prosperity meant having lots of money and belongings; now we know that, no matter our circumstances, prosperity is the experience of thriving with what we have today. We believed that abundance was about getting everything we could for ourselves; we have learned that it is about gratitude for what we have today and generosity toward others. We defined our maturity in terms of the number of credit cards we owned, the salary we made, the positions we held, or the people we employed or supervised; now we define it in terms of the depth of our willingness to practice patience, understanding, and compassion. We used to spend our time and energy in resentment, self-pity, and blame, or in attempting to get out of difficult or embarrassing situations; now we spend it in positive action. We used to have starry-eyed fantasies of some distant future; now we strive to live for today, one day at a time. Our lives were once characterized by the compulsion to debt, and by self-centered fear, self-obsession, and resultant isolation. Our lives were ruled by debts we could not or would not pay. Now they are characterized by genuineness and a desire to be of service, by the integrity that comes with living on a cash basis and paying those we owe, no matter how long it takes.

Such changes did not happen by chance or by adhering to strict self-discipline; nor were they the result of being rescued from the consequences of our debting. They happened through spiritual practice. We came to trust the recovery process and a Higher Power. Our trust might not have been complete at first, but as we continued to move through the Steps, we learned that reliance on a God of our understanding meant serenity, abundance, and freedom. We were transformed. We found a new way to live.

In our experience, there is nothing uniform about spiritual awakening. Each D.A. member has her or his own particular story about how a spiritual awakening came about and what it signifies. One thing most of us share is the realization that we are no longer trying to go it alone. Compulsively living beyond our means kept us focused almost entirely on ourselves. When we considered others, it was often to engage in blame and self-justification. We were mired in isolation, self-obsession, and endless fears. As we continued to practice the Twelve Steps, we found that we were no longer overwhelmed by selfishness. We acknowledged our need for a Power greater than ourselves, for fellowship, and for service to others, perhaps grudgingly at first but with experience showing us time and again that the program works. We were able to keep moving forward. In time, we became truly grateful to have a Higher Power and supportive recovery friends. At our best, we embraced our need for them and were astonished that we had denied ourselves access to this gift for so long.

Does this mean that we are never given to selfishness once we have had a spiritual awakening? Of course not. We are still human. Recovery, like all spiritual growth, is an ongoing process. An essential component of it is reaching out to others; when we are focused on trying to help someone else, we are not obsessively focused on ourselves.

That being the case, the task before us is simple: we try to carry this message to others who might also benefit from it. We have something to offer debtors still suffering from the same compulsion that once ruled our lives. It is vital that we share it, that we open the door of Debtors Anonymous recovery to others and invite them to step through it. We can hold out experience to compulsive debtors, and we can do it from the unique perspective of those who have been in that same desperate place. Many who need D.A. recovery have experienced criticism, judgment, anger, and despair from family and friends, but few have heard the stories of those who once thought, felt, and acted as they have. Our debting history, once such a burden to us, is now transformed into a message of hope for others, just as our gratitude is transformed into the desire to be of service.

Attempting to carry the message is not an afterthought; it is essential to living a life free of compulsive debting. Time and again, D.A. experience has shown that if we take recovery for granted we can easily lose it. We are too prone to becoming preoccupied with self. Every time we relate how the Debtors Anonymous program with the Twelve Steps at its heart changed our lives, we let go of focusing exclusively on ourselves. With humility, we remember that we had been unable to make the necessary changes on our own—or even to know what they were. As we share what we have been given, we renew our willingness and gratitude. Nothing allows us to access the joy of D.A. recovery like sharing the message of our own D.A. recovery.

We always keep in mind, however, that attempting to carry the message of recovery constitutes positive action in and of itself. Certainly we hope wholeheartedly that others will find recovery, but we cannot control outcomes. What we do know is that our efforts, offered with honesty and humility, help ensure our own recovery. Each time we make a point of speaking to a newcomer after a meeting or between meetings, we renew our own commitment. Trying to carry the message keeps us active in and grateful to the D.A. program.

There are many ways to endeavor to carry the message. D.A. meetings present plenty of opportunities. At meetings, we share our experience and our faith in the process of recovery. We can describe how working the Steps changed us once we stopped debting, or how we are applying D.A. principles to our lives, or simply how grateful we are for our recovery. When others speak, we listen; this allows us both to hear the message of recovery and to offer understanding to those who are seeking it. Meetings also provide opportunities for service. We can help set up or clean up D.A. meeting rooms, maintain D.A. conference-call reservations or email groups, restock literature, or take service positions such as group secretary or treasurer. All of these actions carry the message by keeping our meetings healthy and available to the next compulsive debtor who needs them. At the same time, we benefit by staying active in this program that is so essential to our recovery.

Attending meetings ensures that someone will be there for the newcomer. It is vital that we be there to hold out our hands and offer welcome, support, and hope. When a member has relapsed and then returns to the D.A. program, we can be part of encouraging him or her to keep coming back. Meetings present us with opportunities to connect with those seeking pressure relief meetings (PRMs) or sponsorship. These essential forms of service keep the Steps and the Tools alive in our own recovery. When we give PRMs, we pass on our experience of not incurring new unsecured debt, living within our means, and thriving in recovery. Sponsorship enlarges our understanding and practice of the Steps as we guide another member in his or her own Step work. As we do this, we keep in mind that we cannot allow our serenity or self-esteem to be determined by how well or poorly others do in recovery. We attempt to carry the message. Whether and how that message is received is not up to us; it is between that individual and her or his Higher Power.

At some point we realize that we can take our recovery to a new level by volunteering to serve in Intergroup or at the World Service level. Local and international service bodies offer many opportunities to carry the message and share our experiences and gifts, and most members who do so report that they get much more out of it than they give. We welcome the opportunity to see beyond ourselves and our individual needs and to become part of keeping D.A. available, vital, and growing.

Outside of D.A., we keep our eyes and ears open for chances to share about the miracle of our beloved Fellowship. We are sometimes surprised when friends or colleagues open up about financial chaos in their lives, but in time, we come to appreciate these moments as gifts. They offer us yet another occasion to celebrate our delivery from compulsive debting and to make a key difference in another's life as well.

Why do those who have never heard of D.A. turn to us? This often happens because they see the changes in us; our transformation is obvious to them because of how we live our lives. The latter part of the Twelfth Step suggests that we practice these principles in all our affairs. The principles embodied in the Steps have become daily practices.

What are these principles? In Step One, we practiced honesty when we admitted that we were powerless over debt and that our lives had become unmanageable. Step Two embodied hope and faith that a Higher Power could restore us to sanity, while Step Three taught us acceptance of and surrender to that Higher Power's care in our lives. We grew in honesty and courage when we took inventory and shared it in Steps Four and Five. We learned about willingness from Step Six and humility and self-acceptance from Step Seven, while Steps Eight and Nine guided us into forgiveness, freedom, and integrity. In Step Ten, we practiced perseverance and grew in gratitude and honesty as we continued to take inventory and to admit when we were wrong. Step Eleven enlarged our openness and spirituality. Step Twelve brought us to service, D.A.'s greatest gift and best-kept secret. The spiritual growth and the personal fulfillment and joy that countless D.A.s have experienced after committing to service are a testament to this fact.

Now that we have come this far, many of us find it comparatively simple to live these principles within D.A. When we are involved in meetings, pressure relief groups, sponsorship, and service, we have a lot of support in remaining honest, open, and willing and in not incurring new unsecured debt. The true test of our commitment to a spiritual program of recovery occurs outside the program. Working Step Twelve also means practicing D.A. principles in our family and in our social, professional, and financial lives, indeed, anywhere we interact with our fellow human beings. We find that we want to be of service in the world, and we look for opportunities to do so.

The people we were when we got to this program could not have imagined the joy we would find in being of service. We were concerned with satisfying our desires and avoiding any pain or even discomfort. Today we find satisfaction in relying on a Higher Power, living by spiritual principles, and trying to help someone else. As the D.A. Responsibility Pledge reminds us, "I pledge to extend my hand and offer the hope of recovery to anyone who reaches out to Debtors Anonymous."

Our peace of mind does not depend on circumstances; when difficulties arise, we know that we will be guided in responding to them. If we do this work wholeheartedly, we experience the benefits of freedom from compulsive debting one day at a time, and we live truly happy and useful lives in serenity, courage, and wisdom.

*The Twelve Traditions of
Debtors Anonymous*

Tradition One

❧

*Our common welfare should come first; personal
recovery depends upon D.A. unity.*

Our shared history—compulsively living beyond our means, powerlessness over debt and money, and the resulting unmanageability
of our lives—brings us together in Debtors Anonymous (D.A.). What
keeps us together is our shared need for a spiritual solution to our problem
and the desire to gratefully pass on the solvency and spiritual abundance
we have come to experience in D.A. Unity within each D.A. group and
within D.A. as a whole is essential to our recovery. When we work together in unified purpose, recovery is available to each of us. When we
fail to do so, the recovery of every one of us is threatened.

Unity is not uniformity. Except for our shared need for recovery and
our shared solution, we D.A. members are a varied lot. We come from
many backgrounds, cultures, professions, and philosophies. It would be
surprising if we were in constant agreement, and in fact we are not.
Most of our differing viewpoints are easily worked out, but even those
that lead to heated discussions must be reviewed in light of what is best
for all, with our collective focus on the welfare of the group and on the
welfare of the Debtors Anonymous Fellowship.

Every D.A. member who has found recovery has a choice: do the work needed to avoid incurring unsecured debt or return to debting and experience its terrible consequences. To do the work, we need the Fellowship. By extension, because each individual's personal recovery depends upon D.A. unity, each member is responsible for the healthy unity of the Fellowship. If we sacrifice unity for our own desires, we cripple our ability to carry the message to those who still suffer, and risk our personal recovery.

One miracle of recovery is that although we may be very different from our D.A. fellows, we respond to the spiritual message of Tradition One because our need for the program, for each other, and for the newcomer makes us willing to work together. When we remember what is at stake, we are prepared to pull back from divisiveness and control and instead focus on our common concerns and common solution. Thus we ensure that the doors of Debtors Anonymous remain open to all who want what we have.

D.A. offers many resources to help groups foster unity. The Twelve Steps and Twelve Traditions give us a strong body of principles and practices to rely on, so we refer first and foremost to their spiritual and practical guidance. Tradition Four offers specific guidance in considering how our group decisions might affect D.A. worldwide. D.A.'s Conference-approved literature, which offers a wide array of tools and stories concerning debting, recovery, and the D.A. Fellowship, provides a common language and understanding. Although individuals can order books, pamphlets, and other materials from the D.A. General Service Office, having D.A. Conference-approved literature displayed and available at our face-to-face meetings promotes unity by giving members and newcomers greater access to the shared experience, strength, and hope of the Fellowship. D.A.'s online resources, members' participation in local Intergroups, and D.A.'s World Service Conference (WSC) help to keep groups informed about and connected to Debtors Anonymous worldwide. And, of course, we turn to our Higher Power for guidance in moments of confusion, willfulness, or discord, perhaps for the best for everyone involved.

Through using the D.A. Tool of Business Meetings, we both practice and promote group unity. At these (usually monthly) meetings, we consider issues that affect the life and health of the group. When disagreements arise, they are generally addressed in business meetings. Whether these disagreements are simple or complex, collegial or rancorous, our tradition of unity stands us in good stead. Our opinions may vary, and often they do, but as long as we value the gifts of D.A. recovery, attempt to apply the Traditions as a guide to our behavior and decisions, and trust the group conscience, we will find solutions that keep our group vital and unified.

Practicing group unity means taking the focus off ourselves. When we work the Steps, we learn that self-centeredness is a key component of our disease. If we insist on having our own way in a business meeting or in D.A. service, it may well be that our selfishness and our self-centered fear are in play. Through focusing on unity instead of on our individual desires, we move beyond selfishness and into the common good. As we work out a compromise, arrive at a previously unseen option, or simply let go of the outcome, we are working to preserve and strengthen D.A. by acknowledging that something larger than ourselves enriches not only our own lives but the lives of others as well.

Tradition Two

❧

For our group purpose, there is but one ultimate authority—
a loving God as He may express Himself in our group conscience.
Our leaders are but trusted servants; they do not govern.

As individuals in Debtors Anonymous recovery, we learn to listen for the wisdom of a Power greater than ourselves. As D.A. groups, we do the same. So that our groups may grow in unity, we vest final authority not in any one individual but in a Higher Power that speaks through our group conscience. When we truly live by this principle, we are freed from the kinds of power struggles that erode the strength and integrity of so many institutions. We can focus instead on our primary spiritual aim: to stop incurring unsecured debt and to carry the message of recovery to those who still suffer.

One of the gifts of recovery is humility. However certain we may be in our beliefs and opinions, our wisdom remains limited by our individual perspectives. No individual can know for sure what is best for others or for the group as a whole. That is why we rely on a Power greater than ourselves to speak through our group conscience.

How do we describe the Higher Power that guides our group conscience? With one word: loving. Our collective voice emanates from that caring, and we strive to demonstrate caring in our discussions leading to group conscience.

The group conscience process allows a D.A. group or a D.A. service arm to take individual concerns into account, yet reach beyond them to uphold the unity that makes personal recovery possible. A group conscience is not the same as a simple majority vote; rather, it draws on the collective conscience of a group's members, who together reach a level of agreement that we call substantial unanimity. If the group is nearly evenly divided in opinion, a group conscience has not been achieved. The process of reaching group conscience allows individuals the opportunity to offer and hold their opinions. At the same time, if we are in disagreement, it calls upon us all to work toward a group conscience and to accept the group conscience as an expression of Higher Power's guidance and as the best for all, whether or not we can see it at the moment.

Differences of belief and opinion will always exist in D.A. groups and elsewhere. In Debtors Anonymous, we find that when we trust that a loving Higher Power is speaking through our collective voice, we have what we need to accept differences and address whatever issues arise. Regardless of how each of us conceives of a Power greater than ourselves, we have come to rely on it as much in our groups as we do in individual recovery. Whether our Higher Power is deity, spirit, or collective wisdom, whether it is God, Good Orderly Direction, or Group of Debtors, our experience shows that it will see us through.

Group conscience comes into play in the business meetings of our groups, Intergroups, and World Service, including the World Service Conference's and General Service Board's deliberations. For many members, the most immediate context for group conscience is our local groups' regular (typically monthly) business meetings, which address issues and make group decisions that deal with both routine matters and new initiatives. As stated in D.A.'s Tenth Tool, business meetings teach us how Debtors Anonymous operates and help us to become responsible for our recovery. By participating in business meetings, each member has the opportunity to guide the direction of his or her group and contribute to group unity. We also get to experience being part of a functional whole.

When we come to D.A., talk of power and authority is problematic for some of us. We may automatically distrust whomever we think is in charge. This distrust may have resulted from our compulsive debting, or it may have preceded it. However it arose, it can make us suspicious of the motives of group officers and of the process by which decisions are reached. Our distrust may extend to any sort of Higher Power as well. Over time, as we experience the caring that members show one another, we begin to develop faith that the group's trusted servants really are there to give back what they have received, not to tell us what to do. Our faith is further enriched when we see issues raised and resolved in a spirit of cooperation. We see that even conflict does not stop members from caring about each other and the group. We begin to trust in the Higher Power present in the group conscience.

There are times when sensitive issues arise in business meetings. When this happens, some of us may have strong feelings and become controlling or emotionally invested in a particular outcome. This can be unpleasant in the moment, but when we follow our commonly held program principles, we grow both as individuals and as a group. We recall the importance of humility; what we contribute to the group conscience has value, but no more value than the contributions of our fellow D.A. members. We get to speak up about what matters to us, and we get to listen to others as they do the same. We strive to honor all opinions, including those held by a minority of members, and we work to achieve substantial unanimity. We remember that recovery lives in the bonds among us, and we value those more than we value "being right."

Suppose a new member has great enthusiasm for, say, using affirmations. This individual insists that everyone would benefit from the group's creating a list of recovery affirmations and handing it out to members and newcomers. The longer-time members might be tempted to reject this suggestion out of hand. However, the new member and others as well could easily experience the long-timers' reaction as an authoritarian response inconsistent with our Second Tradition. No matter how clear an issue may seem to some members, all decisions that affect the group should be brought to a business meeting. At that time, members can thoughtfully consider the issue, view it in light of the Traditions, and arrive at a group conscience. Instead of each party insisting on the rightness of his or her point of view and the wrongness of its opposite, all can let the collective voice determine what is best for the group, while being mindful of the impact their decision could have on other groups and on the Debtors Anonymous Fellowship.

The group conscience process does need facilitators. At the group level, typically the General Service Representative, the Meeting Secretary, or the Business Meeting Chairperson facilitates the discussions that develop group conscience. At the Intergroup or World Service meetings, the Chairperson of the specific meeting facilitates. Wherever a D.A. group conscience is needed, D.A.'s service principle is the same: our leaders are but trusted servants; they do not govern.

It seems strange to many that we can thrive without a president or other chief executive officer; without a governing body; and without an array of rules, requirements, and prohibitions.[2] However, this is entirely the case in Debtors Anonymous. All those who hold leadership positions, at whatever level, have one common goal: serving the group. They are answerable to, not in authority over, their fellow D.A. members. Individual recovery, group unity, and the D.A. Fellowship as a whole are strengthened by this service.

When we engage in our Eleventh Tool, that of Service, we make every effort to place principles before personalities. One key principle of D.A.

---

2. As a nonprofit organization, Debtors Anonymous must of course have functional legal and financial relationships with non-D.A. entities. Accordingly, as a practical matter, the D.A. General Service Board has clear bylaws and procedures.

service is rotation of leadership. Members rotate into and out of service positions on a regular basis, usually according to the suggested guidelines for length of service found in *The Debtors Anonymous Manual for Service*. Regular rotation of service positions supports the unity we seek in Tradition One, and the group conscience that we follow in Tradition Two; it makes the recovery benefits of D.A.'s Tool of Service available to all. D.A. experience shows that it is not healthy for either the individual or the group when one person holds onto a position for too long. If a person stays overlong in a position, the individual may come to be viewed as the single authority on all matters relating to that position's functions. This is inconsistent with Tradition Two, with the concept of a loving Higher Power as our final authority. Alternatively, the member may become a lightning rod for resentment and conflict, distracting the group from its focus on unity, recovery, and carrying the message. When given the opportunity, we take a service position, we learn to live up to our commitments, and we learn to let go when our term ends. This is a wonderful illustration of the power of recovery for newcomers to D.A., who can see the difference between humble service and controlling governance.

This is not to say that members who step into service have no power. D.A.'s Twelve Concepts entrust officers with the power to serve. When individuals volunteer for D.A. service, they take on specific responsibilities and expectations. Each is supported with the direction and tools needed to fulfill the expectations of that position and is given the power needed to accomplish its duties—in accordance with the group conscience. The Treasurer, for example, is given the responsibility and authority to track the group's monetary inflows and outflows; to make transactions on behalf of the group, including paying expenses according to the group's spending plan; and to make regular reports to the group.[3]

3. *The Debtors Anonymous Manual for Service* outlines suggested duties for each service position, providing guidance for the group and its trusted servants.

Prior to D.A., many of us were inconsistent in living up to our commitments, or we might have failed to do so altogether. Some of us routinely avoided responsibility, or when we did accept it, we did so in a self-aggrandizing fashion without concern for how our actions affected others. There were also those of us who were in such vagueness that we could not even determine what was expected of us.

In D.A., we get to redefine responsibility in terms of service, changing the character of responsibility from burden to gift. We grow spiritually not only by learning to live up to our commitments but by doing so in a manner that contributes to group unity and keeps Debtors Anonymous available to all who seek it. Further, we become trusted servants. When we fulfill our responsibilities to the group, we experience a level of satisfaction and gratitude that is unavailable to us in focusing only on ourselves. How rewarding it is to become worthy of trust! And worthy we are when we faithfully perform the functions of our service positions. Should we fall short, we experience the acceptance and forgiveness of our fellow members as well as the blessing of the opportunity to renew our commitment to our group and to our recovery.

Each member who volunteers for or accepts a service position enriches his or her own recovery, while at the same time working to fulfill D.A.'s primary purpose. When—as Tradition Two invites us to do—we speak with love, listen with openness and humility, maintain clarity, and advocate for the group's greatest good without needing to dominate and without being attached to outcomes, we are honoring the wisdom of a Power greater than ourselves. This is the true spirit of group conscience. When we attend with responsibility to the needs of the group as an essential part of attending to our individual recovery, we are helping to ensure that Debtors Anonymous remains available to the next compulsive debtor seeking help. This is the true spirit of service.

Tradition Three

❧

*The only requirement for D.A. membership is
a desire to stop incurring unsecured debt.*

The sole requirement for membership in Debtors Anonymous is a desire to stop incurring unsecured debt. Many people who do not identify as compulsive debtors have been attracted to and benefited from the Debtors Anonymous program. These include individuals who debt habitually, spend compulsively, shop, underearn, live well below their means, overcommit their time, and so on. Some, after learning more, realize that they are in fact compulsive debtors; for others, the term does not apply.

How can we find unity in this situation? The answer is in D.A.'s Third Tradition. Anyone with the desire to stop incurring debt is fully welcome as a member; our Twelve Steps offer recovery to anyone with the willingness to apply them. Membership in Debtors Anonymous is as simple as that. If we have a desire to stop incurring unsecured debt, we belong. Given that one qualification, we are a member if we say we are. There is no minimum total indebtedness needed to qualify for D.A. membership. Having experienced legal action such as foreclosure or bankruptcy is neither a requirement for nor an impediment to membership. There is no one in D.A. who is going to check our credit record and say that our credit score is too high or too low for D.A. membership. Income level and social status are irrelevant. We may have no income or assets, we may have wealth, or we may fall somewhere in between, and still we can belong to D.A. It does not matter what sort of unsecured debt we incurred in the past. Some D.A. members have used credit cards and others have not; some have taken out student or other signature loans and others have not; some have consistently paid taxes while others are years behind in filing; some have experienced great success at their jobs or in their businesses and others have experienced miserable failure.

Our one membership requirement is designed to be simple in practice and inclusive in spirit. All that we need for a seat at the table, actual or virtual, is a desire to stop incurring unsecured debt. The desire is necessary, and it is also sufficient. We can have the desire without yet having stopped incurring unsecured debt, or without even being fully willing to stop. Our desire brings us to the table, where we can find the necessary willingness to recover.

As members of Debtors Anonymous, we work together to ensure that our groups do not give anyone the impression that there are any other qualifications for membership. We do not adopt policies that supersede the Third Tradition. We avoid any actual or implied hierarchy among members on the basis of income, level of indebtedness, or progress in working the program. Some D.A. members belong to other twelve-step programs or money-related support groups. Such members generally find it necessary to set these experiences aside when sharing in D.A. meetings. Doing so helps prevent confusion for newcomers, who may assume that experience in other programs is part of qualifying for D.A. membership.

Just as we were received with acceptance when we came to D.A., we are called upon to accept others when they reach out to us. Our Fellowship's single qualification reminds us to let go of prejudices and preconceptions about our fellow members and about newcomers. We are not judged, and we do not judge. When we find ourselves wanting to criticize or gossip about others, we talk to our sponsor and practice the Tenth Step. We refocus on our own recovery and on group unity.

We especially do not prejudge newcomers as being unlikely to benefit from D.A. We do not provide service such as sponsorship and pressure relief meetings according to whom we judge to be most deserving. We avoid bias based on race, ethnicity, age, sex, sexual or gender orientation, ability or disability, religion or lack of religion, politics, socioeconomic status, and other such factors. The only important question is whether an individual has the desire to stop incurring unsecured debt. And it is up to each individual to answer that question for him or herself.

What, after all, would be the consequences of denying membership to those who have such a desire and seek our help? Were we to place other restrictions on membership, we would participate in dooming some debtors to all the consequences and misery of continued use of unsecured debt. What might our own lives have looked like if we had come to D.A. and found the door locked against us? What heartbreak would we have caused others and ourselves, and what spiritual guidance and hope would have remained inaccessible? Of course, we might have found another path, and so too might any debtor, but who are we to erect barriers to someone else's recovery?

Once we have the desire to stop incurring unsecured debt, once we say that we belong, we choose to be part of something greater than ourselves. We connect with others and begin to see and hear the similarities among us. Without doubt, we will find many differences as well, but these become less important as we listen for the commonalities and find hope. We recognize that we have been brought together by our common desire and are kept together by the mutual solution found in the Steps, Tools, and Fellowship of Debtors Anonymous. When we declare our desire to stop incurring unsecured debt, we set out on the road to freedom.

Tradition Four

❧

Each group should be autonomous except in matters affecting other groups or D.A. as a whole.

Many of us debtors value independence and do not like being told what to do. In the Fellowship of Debtors Anonymous, we are not told what to do; we are given the opportunity to proceed in our recovery at our own pace and to choose which of the suggested Steps, Tools, and Traditions we will embrace and when. At the same time, we begin to see that we attain the most recovery in our lives when we accept our program's suggestions and our need for interaction with other debtors—regular interaction at meetings and workshops, in pressure relief meetings, in sponsorship, and by phone and the Internet. This interdependence is critical to our recovery and is the antithesis of our pre-D.A. history of unsuccessfully trying to go it alone, often in deep isolation.

Tradition Four tells us that the same is true of our D.A. groups. Autonomy, which is another principle central to the life of any Debtors Anonymous group, is balanced with our responsibility to other groups and the Fellowship as a whole.

In all matters affecting only an individual D.A. group, that group is fully self-governing. Decisions rest with the group conscience. Although group guidelines as expressed in the Traditions, the Concepts, and D.A. service literature, including *The Debtors Anonymous Manual for Service*, provide suggestions that help in making group decisions, each group is free to choose how to implement them. The only exception to this is when group decisions have an impact on other D.A. groups or Debtors Anonymous as a whole.

Each group chooses its meeting location and time, and the specifics of its meeting format, such as how much time is spent on reading, sharing, and so forth. At some meetings, members read and discuss one of the Twelve Steps every week. Other meetings start with a member sharing his or her recovery story, or with members choosing a Tradition, Tool, or other topic for discussion. Still others begin with a reading from D.A. literature and reflection on how it guides recovery. Each group chooses the selection and quantity of its stock of Conference-approved D.A. literature. Each group develops its own spending plan and elects its own trusted servants, and each group may choose how frequently to hold business meetings, how long they are, and how decisions are made.

D.A. groups value their independence, and at the same time, healthy groups recognize their essential interconnection with other D.A. groups and the Fellowship as a whole. Any single D.A. group has much to offer its members and newcomers, but there are ways of serving the members that are beyond the reach of individual groups. Readily visible expressions of this need for interdependence include Intergroup or area fellowship days with D.A. speakers, workshops, pressure relief meetings, and other D.A. recovery activities. In most cases, it takes the service and resources of multiple groups to offer such events. Similarly, creation of literature, a powerful tool for carrying the message of D.A. recovery, is beyond a group's capability. No single group has the resources to write, edit, publish, and distribute program literature; nor does it have access to a group conscience of the entire Fellowship to approve the literature. It takes D.A. as a whole to accomplish that task.

Less visible but equally important, if not more so, is the interdependence groups have with each other and with the worldwide D.A. Fellowship—an interdependence that takes the form of a unified message of recovery from debting no matter where a debtor goes in the world. As such, autonomy does not extend to matters affecting other D.A. groups or the entirety of D.A. Each group needs to be aware of its responsibility not only to itself and its members but to the rest of the Fellowship, and keep its meetings focused on D.A. principles.

If one group were to institute a policy that is widely divergent from D.A.'s suggested guidelines, it could have profound negative effects on how D.A. is perceived and on whether or not those who need recovery would seek us out and trust our experience. For example, a group might decide to adopt membership requirements. Suppose that one group were to declare that only compulsive debtors who used credit cards were welcome at their meetings. Members or newcomers attending the meeting might assume that D.A. is only for those with credit card problems. If they did not fit that description, they might despair of finding help in D.A. This would affect D.A. as a whole and would be in conflict with the Third Tradition.

Similarly, suppose that a group chose to have financial consultants give lectures. These hypothetical speakers might have good information, and D.A. members are as welcome as anyone to seek out such information on their own. However, discussing approaches to money issues that are different from D.A.'s approach might confuse members, especially newcomers, and, possibly to their detriment, they might get the impression that it is D.A. policy to follow the speakers' advice. It would then be an easy leap to blame D.A. for such troubles, damaging D.A.'s public reputation and making it less possible to reach the debtor who still suffers.

D.A. groups that display and read non-Conference-approved literature or allow sharing based on non-Conference approved literature also create confusion and give a misimpression of how D.A. works. Although the outside literature may have great value, its appropriate place is outside D.A. Additionally, individual or local production and distribution of "D.A." literature written by members or local D.A. groups can deeply compromise the Debtors Anonymous message and undermine group and fellowship unity. Further it may give newcomers a skewed perspective of who we are and what we have to offer. Accordingly, it is vital to the integrity and longevity of D.A. that its literature be written and approved through the D.A. World Service Conference literature approval process.

Group autonomy in tandem with keeping the best interests of the larger D.A. Fellowship in mind provides each group with a balance of freedom and responsibility. This balance strengthens the foundation of recovery for all our members and helps us accomplish our primary purpose.

Tradition Five

❧

*Each group has but one primary purpose—to carry
its message to the debtor who still suffers.*

The Fifth Tradition is unambiguous. The message carried by our groups is that there is another way to live; that way is the Twelve Steps of Debtors Anonymous. Every Debtors Anonymous group exists to carry D.A.'s message of hope and recovery to any individual who desires to be liberated from debting. We use every opportunity in our group meetings to share that we have found a spiritual solution to our common problem, and that by living the solution we have ceased incurring new unsecured debt and freed ourselves to move toward the lives we desire. We also make clear that this solution is available to anyone who comes seeking it.

It is vital to the health, and indeed to the very existence, of our groups that we maintain the integrity of our primary purpose. Extending our purpose to other matters would profoundly compromise our ability to carry our twelve-step message of recovery. As such, it is important that we not give the impression that our groups have expertise in anything other than recovery from incurring unsecured debt. There are many outside resources available for those who wish to learn money-management techniques, financial or business strategies, or debt-reduction methods. D.A. has no opinion on these. Instead, we offer something different. This something is a spiritual solution that gets to and releases the spiritual conditions underlying our debting. We offer it specifically to the debtor who still suffers—the individual who chronically fails to live in accordance with his or her means and whose life has thereby become unmanageable.

Anyone who approaches us may well wonder, what's the angle? How does this group benefit from helping someone else? The answer lies in our Twelfth Step. Fulfilling the group's primary purpose is one of the keys to the individual recovery of *every* D.A. member, not just of those who are new. It is absolutely essential that members share on an ongoing basis their experience, strength, and hope with those seeking help because the spiritual path to freedom from compulsive debting does not have an endpoint and relies on sharing our recovery.

Before we came to D.A., we were preoccupied with self. We dwelt constantly on our problems, our fears, and our perceived need for more and more, despite the true costs. Each opportunity to share what we have found in D.A. is a chance to replace our self-centeredness with caring and positive action. This fosters gratitude and humility, which in turn helps ensure ongoing freedom from debting.

When we can say in all earnestness that we have no agenda aside from maintaining our own recovery by trying to share it, our groups are that much more credible as vehicles for helping others with a combination of spiritual and practical actions by which they too can find freedom from debting. Newcomers already know something of the misery of compulsively living beyond their means: the insanity of wanting to stop but not being able to, the financial chaos, the broken relationships, the shame, the self-loathing and despair, perhaps even professional ruin, imprisonment, or suicide attempts. When these newcomers arrive at our group meetings, they learn that we too have been there and have found a way out.

How we share in meetings affects our group's ability to help debtors. Group meetings allow those of us who are no longer incurring new unsecured debt and who have worked the Twelve Steps to tell our recovery stories and explain how using the Steps and Tools has transformed our lives. Even those of us who are early on the path to recovery can inspire others by sharing the progress we are making. We focus on how we recover through the Steps and Tools and how we use the Traditions in all our affairs, rather than dwell on personalities, controversy, socializing, or a long litany of complaints. It is vital that we communicate our experience, strength, and hope. Certainly we may be experiencing difficulties, and we know that honesty is essential to recovery. However, to find hope, the newcomer needs to hear about more than our problems. All members benefit when we balance sharing about our challenges with sharing our spiritual solutions and positive actions.

The time surrounding meetings is equally important. Some groups have a designated greeter or offer a beginners' meeting, but it is every member's responsibility to reach out to those new to the Fellowship and to other members who are struggling. We take time before and after meetings to greet new attendees, visitors, and each other; we invite those who are still suffering to keep coming back. We find that this provides far stronger encouragement than any heavy-handed advice or authority could.

Tradition Five informs the Fellowship's decisions about the content of D.A. literature. In the early days of our Fellowship, it was common to display and sell non-D.A. books at meetings, but much has changed over the years. Today, through the work of the World Service Conference (WSC) and D.A.'s General Service Board (GSB), the Fellowship writes, approves, and publishes a rich body of literature focused on how we debtors stop incurring new unsecured debt and on the spiritual and financial benefits that follow. D.A. also publishes service material in print and online, which reflects guidance from the Traditions, the Concepts, and the GSB and WSC committees.

D.A. experience indicates that displaying books and pamphlets other than those approved by the D.A. WSC is inconsistent with and detrimental to our primary purpose.[4] We have found that promoting outside literature clouds the D.A. message of how we recovered and of what D.A. recovery is. In contrast, Conference-approved literature consistently presents the group conscience of the Fellowship as a whole on what recovery means and how it can be attained.

Outside of our groups, members are, of course, free to use whatever books, websites, workshops, or other resources they find useful. At D.A. meetings, however, the focus is on the Twelve Steps, the Twelve Traditions, the Twelve Tools, and the Twelve Promises.

Our primary purpose serves as a guide and touchstone in our business meetings and in group inventories (a formal process in which a group carries out its own Fourth Step inventory). Each offers an opportunity for members to evaluate whether or not the group is doing all it can to carry the message. If we recognize that we have turned our efforts and resources away from this, we can bring the matter up for a group conscience on solutions. For example, members might voice concerns about what is being shared in meetings. If the focus is entirely on the debts and dramas of each person attending, or if the meeting has become more of a social hour, it is unlikely that the message of recovery is coming through. As a solution, the group might adopt a statement to be read at each meeting, emphasizing the importance of each member sharing the solutions he or she has found in Debtors Anonymous.

Finally, there is a delicate balance between group autonomy as described in our Fourth Tradition and fidelity to our primary purpose. Each group is welcome to run its meetings as its members choose, as long as their choices do not affect other groups or D.A. as a whole. However,

---

4. At the time of this writing, D.A.'s Eighth Tool includes study of Alcoholics Anonymous (A.A.) literature; therefore, A.A. literature such as *Alcoholics Anonymous* and A.A.'s *Twelve Steps and Twelve Traditions* may appropriately be present on a group's literature table.

when a D.A. group loses its focus on our primary purpose, it imperils recovery for members and prospective members alike. As always, clarity and singleness of purpose are our guides.

Help was available for us when we were suffering. As individual members and as D.A. groups, we want and need to provide that same help to others. Staying focused on the core of our program is essential to individual recovery, to D.A unity, to the purpose of our groups, and to keeping Debtors Anonymous a place where those who still suffer can find freedom from the devastation of compulsive or habitual debting.

Tradition Six

*A D.A. group ought never endorse, finance, or lend the D.A.
name to any related facility or outside enterprise, lest problems of money,
property, or prestige divert us from our primary purpose.*

Debtors Anonymous does not exist in a vacuum, nor would it be
desirable for it to do so; it is neither healthy nor practical to isolate
ourselves. At the same time, D.A. takes care to avoid direct or indirect
affiliation with or endorsement of other entities. We do this in order
to remain true to our primary purpose of carrying the message to the
debtor who still suffers. Failing to take such care could easily dilute the
D.A. message and, as Tradition Six states, give rise to divisive conflicts
that could imperil our ability to share what we have gratefully received
in D.A. Tradition One, with its central message of unity, informs all the
Traditions; here it inspires the spirit and practice of Tradition Six.

It does not take much imagination to see that any group of well-
meaning individuals might descend into bickering, infighting, and general divisiveness when money, property, or prestige is at stake; indeed, in
the world at large it happens quite often. It is far too easy to lose focus
and place at risk the very core of a group's purpose when any of these
three elements is involved. How much more so for compulsive debtors,

even for those with years of solvency[5] and years of working the Twelve Steps. Recovery brings sanity and serenity, but it does not make us perfect. Much like the allure of unsecured debt or excessive spending, we debtors could easily be sidetracked by the promise of prestige, the acquisition and maintenance of property, or the draw of outside income. As such, both individual groups and the Fellowship as a whole must always seek to balance vision with humility. Although a misstep or a faltering in our own recovery will not sink the group, the group's aligning itself with an outside cause or organization would be far too likely to divert the group from D.A.'s primary purpose, undermine unity, and even threaten the existence of the group.

Of course, as a single body and as individual groups, Debtors Anonymous must interact with other entities. We cannot hold face-to-face meetings without renting space or offer online meetings without accessing the Internet. Debtors Anonymous General Service Board, Inc. (the Board) is a not-for-profit corporation acting in service to the spiritual Fellowship of Debtors Anonymous. As such, it has legal and fiduciary responsibility for the Fellowship. Accordingly, the Board files tax documents and contracts for various professional services, not the least of which are those associated with our World Service Conference. Tradition Six provides needed guidance on how groups and service arms can conduct necessary business without becoming distracted from our primary goal of carrying the messages.

Clarity is one of our watchwords, and we maintain a commitment to our primary purpose in part by being very clear about nonaffiliation. We avoid not only the substance but the appearance of affiliation or endorsement. When we rent a meeting space, we pay the standard rental rate; failing to do so could suggest an affiliation of ourselves with the community center, clubhouse, or place of worship that provided the space. When we

---

5. In Debtors Anonymous, "solvency" means not incurring new unsecured debt.

speak in meetings, we avoid naming or discussing non-Conference-approved books, specific software packages, companies, institutions, counselors, or coaches so that those new to our Fellowship will not assume that D.A. endorses those products or individuals. Likewise, if we are members of other twelve-step fellowships, we focus our sharing on the D.A. approach, keeping the Debtors Anonymous message clear for all members and visitors. If we have found a great place to buy needed goods at a favorable price, we refrain from mentioning the store's name in the meeting.

Sometimes the principles of Tradition Six strike members or those outside D.A. as too limiting or impractical. D.A. members who, through D.A.'s Steps and Tools, have achieved a spiritual way of life and freedom from incurring unsecured debt are eager to share the D.A. message as freely as possible. They think, "Would it not make sense for our groups to ally themselves with therapists or credit counselors who already refer individuals to D.A., or to contribute money to political candidates who have 'enlightened' views about credit and debt?" Tradition Six does not support such actions. Endorsement or financing of an entity outside D.A. would most likely influence how others viewed Debtors Anonymous, and we cannot afford to alienate those who could receive help from D.A., or who might refer debtors to D.A. because they disagree with the views or practices of outside entities.

Further, if a D.A. group were to accrue money and finance a particular entity and then the entity became embroiled in questionable business practices, D.A.'s reputation could be seriously damaged. If a group endorsed a petition drive to rein in certain credit practices, or lent its name to an advertising campaign warning of the dangers of debt, members of the public might conclude that Debtors Anonymous was an advocacy organization rather than a recovery fellowship whose primary purpose is to help individuals not debt one day at a time. Any of these erroneous perceptions might reduce the likelihood that still-suffering debtors would look to us when they sought help. If we affiliate with other entities, even for the highest of purposes, we place ourselves and our Fellowship at unacceptable risk. Our intentions may be positive, but implementing them holds too high a probability of separating us from one another and from prospective members. Individual members, like anyone else, may choose to become involved in whatever causes they favor, away from their D.A. participation, but they must not use the name of Debtors Anonymous or seek D.A.'s endorsement or financial backing.

Groups and Intergroups have had to address other less obvious challenges to our tradition of nonaffiliation. Every year, Debtors Anonymous groups and Intergroups send general service representatives (GSRs) and Intergroup service representatives (ISRs) to our World Service Conference. The group or Intergroup is responsible for paying the representative's expenses, naturally without incurring unsecured debt. In one area, groups decided to work together to put on a fundraiser, the main attraction of which was to be a non-D.A. speaker; the proceeds of the event would be used to send the representative to the Conference. Some members objected, noting that the event, however well intended, could easily be construed as an endorsement of the speaker's views. Fortunately, the groups agreed and the event was canceled.

Another group followed the Tradition Six principle of non-endorsement by agreeing that any activity that could be construed as self-promotion or promotion of an outside event, such as giving out business cards, flyers, or brochures, could only be conducted at some distance from the room in which the group met, even if the goods or services seemed compatible with D.A. recovery. In any D.A. meeting, the emphasis must be on recovery, not marketing. We are bombarded by marketing outside our meeting rooms and expect respite from sales pitches in our meetings. Knowing that someone may try to sell us something at a D.A. meeting could well be a deterrent to attending.

Tradition Six guides groups in being vigilant about issues of autonomy and outside influence.

Tradition Seven

༄

Every D.A. group ought to be fully self-supporting,
declining outside contributions.

When we discontinue all use of unsecured debt, we become financially responsible, supporting our current needs with current income and assets. This self-support leads to self-respect and is rooted in faith in the Debtors Anonymous program, in a Power greater than ourselves, and indeed gradually in ourselves. Out of gratitude for this transformation and for our meetings, we put money in the basket when it comes around. We also volunteer for service positions when they become available, keeping in mind that self-support isn't just about money.

Because all bodies of our Fellowship are fully self-supporting, it is in the best interests of every D.A. member to contribute according to his or her ability. When we are experiencing prosperity, one way we express gratitude is to give generously at D.A. meetings. Some members send regular individual contributions to the General Service Office (GSO). Large or small, such contributions are included in their spending plan. If we are struggling financially, each contribution we make, regardless of amount, is an act of trust in a Power greater than ourselves.

Similarly, to ensure D.A. continues to be available to us and to others, in addition to our monetary giving we contribute to D.A. through service. Our time and energy make a difference in carrying the message to the still-suffering compulsive debtor and maintaining a healthy program for existing members. If a member's spending plan has little room for Seventh Tradition contributions, the member might consider stepping up his or her service work.

At the group level, during monthly business meetings, groups discuss and decide how they will use the Seventh Tradition funds they have collected. The members receive a report from the Treasurer of inflows and outflows, and they prudently address any issues that could affect the group's financial health. Acting through its Treasurer, the group pays its ongoing meeting expenses, which for face-to-face meetings generally include rent, literature, and whatever supplies the group may require. Telephone or online meetings may pay customary fees for telephone or Internet access.

Above a prudent reserve, which is typically equal to three months' expenses, the group does not retain excess funds. D.A. recommends that the remaining funds be contributed to support the D.A. service structure, in accordance with the group's spending plan and D.A.'s suggested guidelines. At regular intervals, usually monthly or quarterly, the Treasurer sends the group's excess funds to the area's Intergroup and/or the GSO.

In addition to regular Seventh Traditions funds, many groups set aside a percentage of their revenue or pass a second container, for the purpose of collecting funds to send their representative to the annual World Service Conference (WSC).

Functions and activities supported by Intergroups can include hosting fellowship days or workshops, updating area meeting lists, maintaining hotlines or information phone lines, creating and updating local D.A. websites, sending announcements of local D.A. activities, and distributing public information materials. Additionally, some Intergroups support new meetings with seed money for rent and literature, while others provide scholarship funds for attending the WSC.

The GSO, which is frequently the compulsive debtor's first point of contact with D.A., handles many functions that support D.A.'s groups and members. The GSO receives contributions from individuals and groups; fills literature orders; maintains the worldwide list of registered meetings; tracks statistics; responds to telephone, email, and postal inquiries; accomplishes much of the work required to hold the annual WSC; and performs administrative duties to support the General Service Board (GSB) and the Fellowship at large.

These functions require employees, including an office manager, as well as a physical office with the accompanying costs for rent, utilities, equipment, and supplies. Regarding employees, D.A. strives, in the spirit of self-support, to offer compensation that is commensurate with the employees' skills and duties, and it makes every effort to model the principles of financial stability and abundance when constructing the Fellowship's spending plan and paying employees and contractors for their work.

The GSB, which is vested by the groups with administrative and operational authority for the Fellowship, consists of volunteers who perform many hours of service work to support D.A. In coordination with the committees and caucuses of the WSC, the Board oversees development and publication of D.A. literature, including the translation of some literature into languages other than English. The Board also supervises maintenance of the D.A. website, which is a vital resource for debtors worldwide, both those in recovery and those seeking our spiritual solution. The GSB manages the Fellowship's finances, including maintaining adequate financial reserves. As a legal entity accountable to the Fellowship, the Board protects D.A.'s copyrights and ensures that the Fellowship's legal responsibilities toward other entities are fulfilled.

To assist them in conducting these and other functions, the Board hires and pays for professionals, including accountants, lawyers, writers, editors, and graphic designers. Beyond conference calls throughout the year to conduct business, the GSB Trustees meet in person twice a year. The Fellowship is responsible for the travel, food, lodging, and miscellaneous expenses associated with these meetings. All Board functions are supported by our members; we neither solicit nor accept outside contributions.

Finally, the vehicle for capturing the collective will of the Fellowship is the annual World Service Conference, attended by general service representatives (GSRs) and Intergroup service representatives (ISRs) from around the world, plus the GSB Trustees. For most GSRs and ISRs, conference expenses of registration, food, travel, and lodging are paid for by the groups they represent. In addition, during the conference year, the committees and caucuses of the WSC often incur operating and project expenses. These costs are funded from the Fellowship's spending plan, which is developed by the GSB.

As an expression of trust that a Power greater than ourselves is providing for D.A., we take actions in alignment with this belief. D.A.'s groups, Intergroups, and the GSB all track their expenses and formulate spending plans and action plans, which are revised as needed to reflect changing circumstances. Each of these bodies allocates funds to maintain a prudent reserve for covering basic expenses should periods of insufficient income occur.

Given all the activities conducted on behalf of the Fellowship, and the financial costs required to support them, it might indeed be tempting to accept outside contributions. After all, isn't D.A. doing good work in the community, making a difference in the lives of compulsive debtors and reducing the burden placed on the local economy? If a community member or organization wants to support us with financial or material contributions, why not accept them and make the most of it? By refusing such gifts, aren't we acting out of deprivation—saying no to money? The answer to these questions is both spiritual and practical.

Spiritually, were we to accept gifts from outside D.A., it would be far too easy to put our trust in the source of the gifts rather than in a Higher Power. In time, this could very well undermine our prudent practices as well as our spiritual orientation, and cause the Fellowship to lose its way.

Practical reasons also exist to refuse outside contributions. We remember how, when we were compulsively living beyond our means, we put ourselves in positions that left us indebted to others. Then, in our shame over our debting, we sometimes acted from an excessive sense of obligation. As a fellowship, we cannot afford to put D.A. in this position. People who make charitable contributions, especially substantial ones, frequently expect some say in how those monies are spent. However well-meaning, outside individuals or organizations who might contribute to D.A. would not necessarily share our deep commitment to our primary purpose, grasp our spiritual approach to recovery, or understand the factors that lead to compulsive debting. Acquiescing to the influence of such outside contributors would likely compromise our primary purpose, and refusing that influence could cause conflicts that would distract us and draw resources away from our recovery and from carrying the message. Maintaining our financial independence allows us the freedom to focus on what is most important.

We also remember that failing to live by Tradition Seven affects our ability to follow Tradition Six because accepting outside donations may imply endorsement of the person or entity making the contribution. When approached with offers of outside contributions, we express our appreciation, but graciously refuse to accept them. We let the person or organization know that the best contribution they can make to D.A. is to pass on the word that we are here, ready and able to help those seeking a solution to compulsive debting.

Refusing to accept offers of monetary contributions is fairly straight-forward, but there are less obvious situations in which we must also maintain our principle of self-support. Our Intergroups do not advocate for free photocopying, our GSO does not ask for free web hosting, and our Board does not request that accounting or legal services be provided as donations. There are many other examples; the point is that we do not expect or accept outside donations in cash or in kind. We pay our own way.

At the meeting level, what happens when a group is new, has a small membership, or is struggling for some other reason? When a facility offers a free meeting room, does it not make sense to accept it? Not for us debtors. We do not want the owner of the meeting space influencing who might attend our meetings, nor do we want to imply affiliation with the hospital, place of worship, or whatever entity provides the room.

It remains important, even in this situation, to look to the group conscience and a Higher Power for solutions, rather than to a donor. Although each group is autonomous and the final decision does rest with the group conscience, D.A.'s Traditions call upon us to find a self-supporting solution. What many new groups have done is meet in a location that offers free space but then make monthly voluntary contributions as "rent" to the facility. Such contributions might be quite small at first, yet they represent the group's commitment to being self-supporting.

As we do with our individual spending plans, a new group can also begin to establish a prudent reserve right away, even if only a small amount is set aside. Gradually, as meeting donations continue, the group can establish funds for all its basic needs, such as literature and supplies. Other new groups get initial assistance for rent and literature from their Intergroup, when the Intergroup has a spending plan that supports the formation of new D.A. groups.

In D.A., we learn that there is no conflict between money and spiri-tuality or between the expenditure of our time and energy and spirituality. In fact, they are linked. When our financial decisions and service commitments are informed by our spiritual practice—when we "practice these principles in all our affairs"—our individual recovery and the financial and spiritual health of our groups are continuously strengthened, as is our relationship with a Power greater than ourselves. When we act out of trust and gratitude by making monetary contributions and donating our time to take care of the business of D.A., we help keep the doors of Debtors Anonymous open for ourselves and for the next debtor seeking a better way.

Tradition Eight

❧

Debtors Anonymous should remain forever nonprofessional,
but our service centers may employ special workers.

When newcomers make their initial telephone, Internet, or face-to-face contacts with Debtors Anonymous, they often have no idea what to expect. Some are uncertain as to our motivations or assume that we will not understand the pain and desperation of compulsive debting. Once they hear or read about our experiences, they realize that we understand better than anyone because we have been there ourselves. This realization lets newcomers know that they are not alone, helps them let go of shame and blame, gives them hope that they too can find a way out, and opens the door to trusting the process of recovery.

The fact that we as debtors are experts only on our own story of debting and recovery is essential to our being able to help newcomers and other members. It is our debting and recovery experience alone that makes us useful. Everything we provide we offer in a spirit of service and with the knowledge that we keep what we have by giving it away. Our only compensation takes the form of continuing recovery and spiritual growth. No one is ever paid to act as a trusted servant or to be a sponsor or to participate in pressure relief meetings. This distinguishes D.A. from non-twelve-step entities that charge for financial or counseling services. Paying members to do twelve-step work could compromise our unity and interfere with developing the humility called for in our Seventh Step and in all our Traditions. It could create differences in status between paid and unpaid D.A. members, and between those who could afford services and those who could not. It could cause dissension about who gets paid and how much. Such divisions would be inconsistent with the spirit of humility, equality, and gratitude that is fundamental to our recovery. In addition, many of us find issues of social class and economic status challenging enough outside D.A.; we do not want to foster these tensions within our Fellowship as well.

Our tradition of nonprofessionalism also creates safe boundaries for members whose professions in finance, law, mental health, and other disciplines touch on D.A. challenges and recovery. Within the Fellowship, each of us, including professionals, is first and foremost a debtor and a member of D.A. Accordingly, these professionals typically find it essential to their own recovery to "leave it at the door" and refrain from shifting the focus from their recovery to their particular expertise. This combination of freedom and humility provides the opportunity for any compulsive debtor, regardless of profession or status, to find a home in D.A. This too fosters equality and unity because no one is seen as more of an expert than another, and debates are avoided about whose outside expertise is better or more correct.

Tradition Eight allows D.A. to employ special workers to support the Fellowship's service functions. D.A. makes various contractual arrangements such as those for legal, accounting, and writing services. D.A. has employees who carry out key functions such as administration of the General Service Office (GSO). This has been important to the growth of Debtors Anonymous. At one time, such centralized functions of D.A. as filling literature orders and answering inquiries were handled entirely by volunteers. Over time, it became clear that there were too few people trying to handle too much, hampering our ability to respond to the needs of our groups and those seeking help. D.A. then opened an office and hired a part-time office manager. Further growth and careful planning eventually allowed the hiring of a full-time office manager for the GSO. Similarly, all of the writing of Debtors Anonymous literature was once done by volunteers. Later, D.A. began contracting with authors who were also members of D.A. to write specific books and pamphlets. This contracting of professional services has allowed D.A. to steadily generate a growing body of recovery literature.

Only a couple of tasks require that a D.A. employee be a member of Debtors Anonymous. One involves first contact with prospective members, such as answering telephone calls and online inquiries received by the GSO from newcomers. Another is writing or editing D.A. literature. Because the literature embodies the D.A. program, it needs to be produced by people who have experienced D.A. recovery. For all other positions, the paid worker need only have the appropriate skills for the job.

For D.A. members who are also D.A. employees or contractors, it is important, of course, to distinguish between professional duties and personal recovery. Without question, an employee's fulfillment of his or her duties is of benefit to the still-suffering debtor, just as service work is. The employee is, however, not paid to provide service work, but only to carry out the responsibilities of the paid job. It is also important for the worker to stay in the spiritual space of "just another debtor" outside the confines of the paid job. And, of course, the job does not replace meetings or recovery service.

The Fellowship's having paid employees and contract workers does not eliminate the need for D.A. members to provide service at all levels, including volunteering at the GSO. (If we live near the GSO, we can set up a volunteer schedule. If we are ever visiting the area, we can drop in to help out for an hour or two.) Debtors Anonymous would likely cease to exist without its members' service, both for lack of hands to do the work and because members would not be able to complete their Twelfth Step of recovery.

The Fellowship of Debtors Anonymous is a strong, interdependent body. By its remaining nonprofessional, each of us can gratefully nurture the spiritual growth that is possible when we stop incurring new unsecured debt one day at a time. Each new person who seeks relief from the burden of debt and debting discovers that we are here solely to receive and pass on the gift of recovery, that all our service activities support this purpose, and that every recovering member is enriched by offering the gift of recovery to others.

Tradition Nine

❧

*D.A., as such, ought never be organized; but we may create service
boards or committees directly responsible to those they serve.*

Organization is a key feature of most institutions, whether they are
governmental, academic, corporate, or charitable. Every institution has its rules and structures, its policies and procedures, its chain of
authority and accountability. Most function in a top-down fashion, with
those at higher levels in the organization directing those below them.
Relationships between individuals, offices, and divisions are explicitly
spelled out or implicitly understood. Those in authority have consider-
able power to determine the direction, and thereby often the success, of
the institution.

Debtors Anonymous is not structured in this hierarchical manner;
instead, the Fellowship functions in a bottom-up fashion. This is clearly
expressed in our Twelve Concepts for D.A. World Service, which guide
the Fellowship as a whole much as the Twelve Steps guide individual recovery and the Twelve Traditions guide group unity. Concept One states:
"The ultimate responsibility and authority for Debtors Anonymous
World Services should always remain with the collective conscience of
our whole Fellowship as expressed through the D.A. groups," meaning

that the group conscience of its members guides the direction of D.A. and the actions of its Board. We of Debtors Anonymous do not claim that this way of doing things is superior; we only say that it works for us.

It is not practical for D.A. members and groups to sustain all the functions involved in carrying the message. Some activities must be centralized, so we form Intergroups, which connect groups by geographical area or medium, and we maintain a World Service Conference (WSC), a General Service Board (GSB) comprising volunteer debtor trustees and nondebting trustees, and a General Service Office (GSO). Each of these, in turn, has committees and subcommittees to carry out the work of the Fellowship. As a legal entity, the Board has bylaws, which define its makeup and working methods much as The Debtors Anonymous Charter defines and guides the processes of the World Service Conference. [6] Yet all bodies have final accountability to the individual members and groups of Debtors Anonymous.

By sending representatives to the annual WSC, groups and Intergroups participate in distinguishing the collective conscience that guides the work of the Board. These general service representatives (GSRs) and Intergroup service representatives (ISRs) make sure that their groups are informed about the issues facing D.A. as a whole and are responsible for expressing the will of the groups during the proceedings of the WSC. Individual members can submit to the GSO ideas and areas of concern, which are distributed to the committees for discussion and group conscience at the next WSC. The Board then exercises oversight on overall policy, finance, and custodial matters to carry out the will of the Fellowship as expressed at the WSC, while delegating everyday management to the GSO. Throughout all this, Debtors Anonymous is guided by its primary purpose, by its Traditions and Concepts, and by a Higher Power as expressed in our group conscience.

6. More information on the GSB bylaws and D.A. service structure is available in *The Debtors Anonymous Manual for Service*, which can be ordered from the GSO or viewed on D.A.'s website.

Although we have guidelines, bylaws, and a charter, we avoid any rules, conditions, or exertion or appearance of authority that might deter anyone who is seeking recovery. One way we do this is by rotating members into and out of service positions. Everyone benefits from this practice because all members remain on an equal footing with no special authority. Rotation also helps our Fellowship remain vital as the work of D.A. continues. Our groups, Intergroups, GSB, and WSC benefit greatly from the variety of experience levels and perspectives afforded by rotation.

Though some might expect this arrangement to result in chaos, that has not been our experience. We have learned that for our purposes it is not a system of strict rules and attendant rewards and punishments that prevents chaos; rather, it is our singleness of purpose. We have been freed from the compulsion to debt, and our deep gratitude, coupled with the knowledge of our lives before D.A., fuels our desire to work together for the good of the Fellowship and the still-suffering debtor.

The D.A. service structure has direct responsibility to those it serves. This creates a kind of reciprocal responsibility, with each of us members having a responsibility to voice any concerns we may have about divergence from D.A. principles. If we see a meeting or committee acting in a way or making decisions not consistent with our Traditions or Concepts, we bring it to the attention of the collective conscience for due consideration, typically by way of a group or Intergroup business meeting or, at the World Service level, through the Issues and Concerns process. We have no need for stringent rules or for mechanisms to enforce them, but we do keep each other honest, as individuals, groups, and service boards.

Just as the aim of each D.A. member is individual recovery and carrying the message, the aim of each service board and committee is to ensure that recovery is within reach of those who seek it. Our primary purpose is carried out daily at every level of service, creating an ever-widening circle of recovery.

Tradition Ten

◈

*Debtors Anonymous has no opinion on outside issues; hence the
D.A. name ought never be drawn into public controversy.*

Debtors Anonymous exists to help debtors attain and maintain recovery from debting. By preserving our unity and remaining committed to our primary purpose, we are able to offer our tried-and-true
approach to debtors driven to desperation—an approach that leads to
the sanity and serenity that are possible when we stop incurring new
unsecured debt.

The gift of twelve-step recovery is precious to each of us, so we share
it freely and guard it carefully. One way to safeguard our program—to
keep it viable and vibrant—is to avoid involving our Fellowship in outside issues. Guided by Tradition Ten, we take great care to avoid having
D.A. become embroiled in contention, as could occur if we allowed any
part of the D.A. Fellowship to become involved in public controversy.

Conflict in human affairs is inevitable. No two of us see the world
in exactly the same way, and most of us believe that our way of seeing
is right and good. Even trivial disagreements can result in significant
conflicts; the higher the stakes, the more we tend to defend our own
views. It would be far too easy to generate rancor within our Fellow-

ship if the General Service Board, the World Service Conference, or our Intergroups were to take a public stand on any outside issue, especially a controversial one, and of course we never know what is controversial to someone else. Likewise, we might bring ourselves into conflict with non-D.A. entities, resulting in ill will or bad press. We cannot afford to do this, because D.A's ability to help debtors depends on its being neutral territory, where people of all social and political opinions can gather to solve their common debting problem. Additionally, in dealing with such conflicts, we would have to turn our attention away from our primary purpose, risking both our own recovery and our usefulness to others.

Further, conflict may bring with it a desire to control, to make things work out the way we think they should. This is in direct opposition to Tradition Two, which reminds our groups that a loving Higher Power as expressed in our group conscience is our only authority.

One might suggest that there are outside issues on which the D.A. Fellowship could find unity. D.A. might be tempted to provide opinions on lending practices, government finances, investing, or other financial topics. Would it not be beneficial for a D.A. group or D.A. as a whole to offer an informed and eloquent opinion that might sway policymakers? Surely this could be a way to have a voice in improving many lives, while at the same time raising the profile of Debtors Anonymous and attracting more members. Perhaps at first glance such action might seem desirable, but looking more closely, we see many pitfalls.

Some who do not agree with a public statement made in the name of the D.A. Fellowship might in frustration give up on D.A., only to find themselves without the support they need to avoid compulsive debting. Others might want to express their differing viewpoints in meetings, which could create conflict and in any event would draw attention from the pursuit of a spiritual solution to our common problem. What about newcomers who look to D.A. for help and find its members arguing with each other about things that have nothing to do with recovery from debting? The experience, strength, and hope that they need and want could be lost in struggles for power and control. Similarly, those seeking help might never even give D.A. a try because they don't agree with a position the Fellowship took publicly on an outside issue. Finally, any money, time, or energy that we might devote to outside issues would distract us from our primary purpose instead of appropriately directing our resources to carrying the D.A. message to those who still suffer. Potential disruption in our sharing the message of hope and recovery far outweighs any good that the Fellowship might do by taking a public stand on an issue.

D.A. membership does not limit anyone's individual right or ability to have opinions or take on causes. In fact, recovery gives us members more confidence and strength to speak up about, work for, or contribute to whatever we deem important. We just need to remember that such actions should not be joined with the name of Debtors Anonymous or be undertaken within our meetings, where we would be imposing our views on people who were seeking recovery.

As individuals and as groups, we also need to avoid the subtler manifestations of injecting outside issues into our sharing at meetings. For example, a member might refer to his or her beliefs on an outside issue, such as a religious tenet, political viewpoint, or financial program. Regardless of the intent of the person, with this expression of opinion, other individuals may feel uncomfortable or unsafe because the outside issue being referenced is in conflict with their own beliefs.

If we find ourselves confronted with outside issues, we can let go of such distractions when we respond by bringing our focus back to D.A.'s Steps, Traditions, and Tools. Keeping in mind the newcomer or struggling member in the room, we refocus on recovery—our experience, strength, and hope—to create a safe, respectful, and welcoming place for anyone seeking relief from compulsive debting.

Tradition Eleven

❧

*Our public relations policy is based on attraction
rather than promotion; we need always maintain personal
anonymity at the level of press, radio, and films.*

Anonymity and attraction without promotion constitute the foundation of the Debtors Anonymous public relations policy. We members observe anonymity; that is, we do not reveal both our identity and our membership in D.A. at the level of press, TV, radio, films, the Internet (including social media viewable by the public), or any other public medium developed after this writing. Public outreach is necessary if we intend D.A.'s message of hope to reach as many debtors as possible. Those who still suffer from compulsive or chronic debting cannot find us if they have never heard of D.A.

Our Eleventh Tradition is so important that it has been the subject of much consideration by Debtors Anonymous service bodies, resulting in publication of *The Public Information Manual for Debtors Anonymous*, a guide for outreach, including via media and through institutions such as hospitals and correctional facilities. The guide is available in print and on the D.A. website. *The Debtors Anonymous Manual for Service* also includes Public Information (PI) guidance. This clear public relations policy allows us to share the D.A. message while protecting D.A. from possible adverse effects arising from misinformation or misjudgment on the part of a well-intentioned individual member.

To further support carrying the message outside of D.A., the General Service Board's (GSB) PI Committee offers media contact training and informational sessions in person or remotely to interested members of the Fellowship. A member who has studied the PI manual, has taken the training, and is prepared to practice D.A.'s PI guidelines can serve as a group's or Intergroup's Public Information Representative (PIR) and interact with the media to attract individuals to D.A.

There are many places and channels for attracting those who can benefit from D.A. Trained PIRs might staff booths at health fairs or conferences. Groups often publish their meeting times and locations in print and online community calendars. They may arrange for a public service announcement with local radio stations. Intergroups can contact area professionals such as psychotherapists and employee assistance counselors to inform them about D.A. and where to find local meetings. Outreach can be made to credit counseling services, suggesting referral to D.A. of those people whose finances are so stressed they are not accepted into the credit counseling program. The list is as long as our ingenuity; we can initiate any outreach that can be made by attraction, without implication of affiliation or endorsement, and with anonymity if media is involved.

Of course, some PI activities require in-person contact and identifying ourselves as members of D.A. This is fine when getting permission to post a flyer, say, at our local library, but we do not necessarily have to give our names and certainly not our last names. Being asked for our last name in such circumstances could be an opportunity to explain anonymity, one of the most attractive aspects of our program. We do, however, as noted, observe anonymity in all contacts with media, whether written, auditory, or visual. We can use all media to offer information about our Fellowship and our meetings, but we do not associate this information with individual members. If appearing on TV or in a podcast, for example, members do not allow recognizable images of themselves to be projected. If a member has an unusual, identifiable voice, voice masking should be employed.

A member might consider it important for a variety of reasons to tell his or her story via some public medium. This does not conflict with Tradition Eleven as long as the member does not mention Debtors Anonymous by name or reveal his or her membership directly or indirectly, for example by referring to "a debt-related twelve-step program."

The distinction between attraction and promotion can be subtle and at times hard to make. Bringing Debtors Anonymous to visibility and providing some basic information about the program—anonymity, the absence of membership fees, the fact that we offer a common solution that draws on our collective recovery experience, and the like—is enough to allow attraction to happen. (In sharing about the program, we can rely on the PI manual and the principles in the Steps and Traditions.) In contrast, promotion tries to sell D.A.'s value and tries to get a person to join D.A. Even within our Fellowship, we practice attraction. We make announcements about D.A. events, but we don't give a sales pitch to promote them.

One potentially harmful type of promotion occurs when members engage in "marketing" D.A. by making extravagant claims, such as asserting D.A. will lead to a good credit rating or personal wealth or other specific outcomes. Hearing these assurances, newcomers seeking quick relief might abandon their D.A. involvement if they do not receive such results or do not get them quickly. Similarly, the promise of easy resolution of debt could promote D.A., but it would be misleading and disappointing. When the debtor learns that getting out of debt means no longer incurring unsecured debt and covering current needs first before debt repayment, his or her expectations will not be met and he or she might tell others that "D.A. doesn't work." Further, potential members might associate Debtors Anonymous with outside enterprises that deal in debt reduction, both reputable agencies and those that exploit their clients. Such association, however mistaken, could compromise our ability to fulfill each group's primary purpose: to carry its message to the debtor who still suffers.

Promoting D.A. with "silver bullet" promises is inconsistent with the nature of D.A. recovery. When we were compulsively living beyond our means, we were often looking for the quick fix. We used debt to get what we wanted when we wanted it, heedless of our true needs and careless of the welfare of others. When we created problems through our debting, we looked for the easy way out and took it whenever possible. Once we started D.A., we had to abandon the quick fix. Working the Steps, implementing Tools such as recordkeeping and a spending plan, gradually paying down our past unsecured debt, and becoming less fearful and more comfortable in our own skin happened through steady application of program principles over time. So it is with D.A. outreach: spreading the word about Debtors Anonymous and growing its membership is a gradual process of attraction.

Another similarity exists between our personal recovery and our PI efforts. Just as recovery from debting in D.A. is not accomplished alone, attracting debtors to D.A. is a shared endeavor achieved through the efforts of D.A. members working together. This is accomplished by applying the wisdom of the program as expressed in the PI manual and sticking to recommended methods of sharing about D.A. Appointing oneself a public spokesperson for the Fellowship and expressing one's personal views on the program could be as perilous for the speaker as for D.A. In addition to perhaps giving a skewed idea of the program, it could lead to compromise of the member's focus on D.A.'s spiritual principles; humility could easily give way to pride, and honesty to the drive to look good.

Members of our Fellowship who are in the public eye might seem well placed to increase D.A.'s visibility, but this too might backfire. Although a celebrity "spokesperson" might attract many to Debtors Anonymous, the message might be too closely associated with that particular person. If the celebrity took a contentious stand on an outside issue or experienced a relapse visible to the public, our Fellowship's reputation could be compromised. Again, D.A. cannot afford to let its mission or success rise and fall on the personality or wisdom of any individual or group of individuals.

Of course, any member can be of service to individuals outside the Fellowship by privately sharing his or her D.A. experience. Although anonymity at the public level is vital, whether or not to remain anonymous at the personal level is an individual choice. Many of our members have found themselves in a position to introduce Debtors Anonymous to others who might benefit from it. The principle of attraction rather than promotion applies in these private conversations as well. We do not lecture, nor do we make demands or guarantees. When we ourselves were deep into our compulsive debting, we typically closed our minds if someone said to us, "When are you going to grow up and live by a budget?" or "Your money problems are so bad, you really should get some help." As recovering debtors, we respect the right of others to choose for themselves if and how they seek help. All we offer is our own stories, without judgment or advice. In the end, the sum of our experience, strength, and hope as manifested in our changed behavior and outlook is the best outreach we can offer.

Tradition Twelve

Anonymity is the spiritual foundation of all our traditions,
ever reminding us to place principles before personalities.

As we arrive at the Twelfth Tradition of Debtors Anonymous, we are reminded of the fundamental spiritual character and basis of all our Traditions, much in the same way our Twelfth Step reminds us that our journey through the Steps is a spiritual one. Tradition Twelve not only identifies anonymity as the basis of all of the Traditions, it also gives us the key to understanding and applying the spiritual concept as we strive to follow the Traditions in D.A. and in all our affairs. The key is placing principles before personalities.

When we voluntarily choose to be guided by the Traditions, we are led, time and again, to placing principles before personalities. We begin to see that doing so is an act of humility. We grasp that all the Traditions—from our acknowledgment in Tradition One that our common welfare comes first, through our relinquishment of personal recognition in Tradition Eleven—call for replacement of self-centeredness with action for the common good, which in turn produces an understanding of humility and our place in the universe. Our Steps and Traditions remind us that recovery from compulsive debting is not about any one individual, but about all of us working together. This willingness of each member to let go of personal recognition for the sake of our primary purpose illustrates the spiritual nature of the D.A. program.

Anonymity has multiple meanings and applications in Debtors Anonymous. The most widely known meaning, confidentiality, is usually the most important to new members. Anonymity expressed as confidentiality means that a debtor can attend a D.A. meeting without revealing his or her full name (or even first name, for that matter), become a member, keep such membership private, and expect that his or her personal story, debting history, and path to recovery will be held in confidence.

Many of us, when we first come to D.A., are afraid of being judged. Typical of our pre-D.A. practice of keeping secrets, we do not want anyone to know about the consequences of our compulsive behavior. After a while, we are reassured by the anonymous nature of the Fellowship. We are grateful that members observe anonymity and unity, that who we are and what we say stays within the group, and that members do not engage in gossip.

By not discussing outside of the meeting, either in well-intentioned comment or judgmental gossip, who we see or what is said, we are honoring an important principle of recovery: we are protecting the anonymity of other meeting participants—as we would want done for ourselves—and we are helping to ensure the integrity and health of the meeting.

As we continue to participate in D.A. meetings, we learn that the mutual assurance of anonymity not only creates a safe environment but also emphasizes that every D.A. member is equally valued. Humility and anonymity help keep our focus on group unity and our common welfare. What matters is not who our fellow members are, how much they have, or even whether or not we like them. What matters is that we all share in the desire to recover.

Some of us choose to let family, friends, and colleagues know about our involvement in the Fellowship. Others prefer to keep it private or to share it only in specific situations. The confidentiality aspect of anonymity can be highly important, if not critical, to members who work in a financial industry or have fiduciary responsibility in their jobs, whether running a cash register at a convenience store or serving as an officer of a large organization. These members, if known publicly as debtors, could well be seen as untrustworthy by people who do not understand that very frequently even unrecovered debtors are completely reliable in their work—making a mess only of their own finances—or who do not understand that debtors recovering in D.A. often become some of the most fiscally responsible of people.

As a result of our recovery, others may see the changes in our lives and be attracted to our new spiritual focus. When this occurs, we remember that anonymity is not secrecy. On a one-to-one level, individual D.A. members are welcome to share their recovery with whomever they deem appropriate. Indeed, nothing speaks as strongly to the power of D.A. recovery as each member's experience. So, when we find ourselves in the right place at the right time to be of service to someone else, we freely share our story of recovery in Debtors Anonymous, letting the person know what D.A. is and what it has done for us. In our sharing, the credit for our recovery goes primarily to the Fellowship, to our Higher Power, and to the spiritual principles that made it possible for us to stop debting when our individual efforts had failed.

This is the kind of humility—being willing to reveal ourselves to help another and give credit to the Fellowship for our recovery—that is essential to our spiritual growth. When we, as individuals or groups, lack such humility, we are in danger of losing our spiritual footing. For example, when our lives begin to turn around, if we become arrogant about how well we are doing, possibly even claiming our progress as evidence of a higher order of spirituality, our recovery is at grave risk. This ego-driven thinking is the precise opposite of anonymity and is how we thought when we were compulsively debting. Similarly, D.A. groups that lose sight of anonymity as humility may risk their ability to help existing and prospective members. This can occur when a group exercises autonomy inappropriately in the belief that their meeting is more in the know than the group conscience of the Fellowship.

In meetings, we practice humility by sharing our own experience. No member acts as a spokesperson for the group or for the D.A. Fellowship. As such, we avoid statements that begin "we all agree" and avoid a lecturing stance and phrases like "you should." This humility is as important when we give pressure relief meetings and meet with sponsees as it is when we share in our home group or on a D.A. service committee.

In spiritual terms, the essence of anonymity is humility. In taking the Twelve Steps, we come to understand that humility does not mean inferiority; we find instead that to be humble is to be teachable and to be open. Anonymity as humility means that no one of us is more or less valuable than any other. Each of us is a debtor among debtors. Our practice of anonymity allows each person to find a place within Debtors Anonymous. As newcomers, some of us do not wish to speak or receive any special attention at our first meetings; if we choose not to say anything at all, that is respected. We are all free to approach the program and recovery in ways that fit for us.

Anonymity and the humility it evokes remind us that our recovery depends on the experiences of others who work the program of Debtors Anonymous. We recognize that it is a privilege to be entrusted with other members' experiences. Within D.A., we are all compulsive debtors who would be lost without one another. We show this clearly when we express our gratitude for and to the Debtors Anonymous Fellowship, a Power greater than ourselves, and our fellow D.A. members. When we share our recovery with gratitude, emphasizing recovery principles rather than individual accomplishment, we are demonstrating the spiritual nature of anonymity, placing principles before personalities.

*The Twelve Concepts of
Debtors Anonymous*

Concept One

༚

The ultimate responsibility and authority for Debtors Anonymous World Services should always remain with the collective conscience of our whole Fellowship as expressed through the D.A. groups.

This Concept recognizes the fundamental fact that all authority in D.A. flows through the groups and their members. As the Second Tradition recognizes, the ultimate authority in D.A. is a loving God as expressed in our group conscience. The groups are the primary interpreters and discerners of the Higher Power's will for the future of D.A. They remain at the top of the "inverted triangle," which represents the D.A. service structure. It is they who select the general service representatives (GSRs) and who create the Intergroups represented by Intergroup service representatives (ISRs) who attend the annual World Service Conference. The groups retain the power to discipline all elements of D.A. service through their control of D.A.'s finances. Since D.A. is constrained by the Seventh Tradition from seeking outside funding, ultimately the groups provide the source of D.A.'s income, either directly through group contributions or indirectly through group purchases of literature.

It is because the groups retain this ultimate authority that the positions of GSR and ISR are so important in D.A. It becomes necessary that a communications link exist to express that authority, and the GSRs and ISRs are that link. In consequence, it becomes vital for the GSRs to listen carefully to their individual group members and the conscience of the group as a whole as expressed at business meetings. Only if GSRs or ISRs are informed of the group conscience can they carry that under-standing beyond the group level to the World Service Conference. It is equally important that these representatives ensure that their groups are fully informed of the facts upon which these decisions are based. Thus, it is their responsibility to report back to the members all information relevant to the World Service structure.

The groups cannot exercise this responsibility and authority by them-selves. They must act through the World Service Conference, composed of GSRs, ISRs, Trustees, and appropriate office staff.

The watchword for this Concept is responsibility. Groups and their members must act responsibly in learning about issues that affect D.A. as a whole and in exploring the possibilities for D.A.'s future. Often groups resist providing adequate time to their GSR to report back on matters of general importance. This is one of the most obvious ways in which groups disregard Concept One through lack of awareness. Responsibility to keep the group informed also rests upon the GSR or ISR. Information flows both ways via the GSR or ISR. It is that person's duty to represent the group and attempt to express its conscience. If GSRs fail to recognize their responsibility to discern the group conscience, they are tempted to act as if they are the ultimate arbiters, failing to consult and listen. Equally important, the GSR has the obligation to report back to the group on his or her decisions and votes and to accept criticism gracefully if there has been a failure to listen.

Concept Two

❧

*The D.A. groups have delegated complete administrative and
operational authority to the General Service Board.
The groups have made the Conference the voice and conscience
for the whole Fellowship, excepting for any change in the Twelve
Steps, Twelve Traditions, and in Article 10 (the General
Warranties) of the Conference Charter.*

The idea of trust is basic to this Concept. It informs us that the
groups have made the decision to place their trust in the World
Service Conference and the General Service Board (GSB) to make the
best decisions for the Fellowship in all matters of administration and
operation of D.A. The Second Tradition points out that our leaders are
"trusted servants." They do not order or direct groups or their members.
Instead, they are to listen to and try to carry out the will of the groups,
receiving the trust of its members to discern the best ways—within the
context of the Steps, Traditions, and Concepts—to implement that will.
Under this Concept, the General Service Board, members of which are
known as Trustees, is given great freedom and flexibility in carrying out
the business of the D.A. Fellowship. The Board has the corresponding
obligation to act carefully and prudently.

It is obvious that, in most matters, the groups can directly exercise neither policy-making nor operational authority in implementing the group conscience. Because of this, Concept Two maintains that the groups must act through the Conference, which they have made the voice and conscience of the whole Fellowship. This Concept thus establishes trust of the Conference to act in a way that represents the informed opinions of the groups and their members.

As Concept Eight states, primary leadership in overall policy matters rests with the General Service Board. However, leadership that acts without listening to advice is neither wise nor prudent. Since the Conference is the collective voice and conscience of the Fellowship, the Board has an obligation to listen to and to heed that advice, in all but the most extreme cases. (For example, when the Conference adopted a motion to direct how outside literature should be used at meetings, the GSB refused to implement this directive on the ground that it violated several Traditions.) In general, duty calls whenever the Conference acts with substantial unanimity, that is, by a two-thirds vote. Even in those cases where the Conference is unable to muster a two-thirds vote for a course of action, the General Service Board has the duty to listen to the opinions expressed and, in appropriate cases, to moderate or change course to reflect what has been discussed.

In three areas, however, the groups have retained their authority over the Conference and General Service Board. These matters are regarded as so basic to the D.A. program of recovery, to D.A. unity, and to the effectiveness of service that no action should be taken without the expressed consent of the groups. These three areas are changes to the Twelve Steps, the Twelve Traditions, and Article 10 (the General Warranties) of the Conference Charter. Here, the Conference Charter recognizes that the World Service Conference may not act to change these fundamental principles unless three-quarters of the D.A. groups grant their permission to do so.

Concept Three

❦

*As a traditional means of creating and maintaining a clearly defined
working relationship between the groups, the World Service Conference,
and the Debtors Anonymous General Service Board, it is suggested
that we endow these elements of world service with a traditional
"Right of Decision" in order to ensure effective leadership.*

The "Right of Decision" refers to the right of every person in service
to act in accordance with her or his best understanding of the will
of the Higher Power in carrying out assigned duties. Except in the most
extreme cases, such as a paid General Service Office employee refusing
to carry out the direct instructions of the General Service Board (GSB),
each member of D.A. is answerable to his or her own conscience. Again,
the ideal of "trusting our trusted servants" plays a role.

Even more important in understanding this Concept is the idea of
honesty. The Right of Decision can be exercised only in the context of a
true dedication to honesty in all things. Each person seeking to exercise
this right must perform a thorough examination of conscience and an
honest evaluation of motive. All too often, what seems at first glance
like a prompting of principle turns out to be an exercise in rationaliza-
tion. Motives such as pride or anger can be disguised in the cloak of this

Concept. Sometimes our character defects like sloth or a desire to please prompt our actions.

The Right of Decision is exercised most frequently by the GSR or ISR. A GSR who has actively sought out the conscience of the group and who comes to the Conference with a clear idea of what the group wants may be presented with new facts or arguments that did not occur to the group's members in their discussion. The GSR may learn of needs of other groups or regions of the country or world that the group did not consider. In such a case, the GSR may appropriately exercise the Right of Decision to reach a conclusion different from that of the group and vote contrary to the group's direction. In doing so, the person exercising that right must be prepared to justify his or her actions to the group.

However, the right applies to all levels of service. Thus a group officer has the Right of Decision in carrying out the functions of the office she or he occupies. At the most mundane level, the group setup person has the right to choose the cookies to be served. At a more important level, the group Chair has both the duty and right to prevent an individual from disrupting a meeting in progress. In each case, the decision maker must operate within the constraints of delegated authority: if the group has determined that chocolate cookies must be served, the setup person cannot choose to serve lemon cookies; the Chair cannot ban an individual from group meetings without consulting both the group and the Third Tradition.

Similarly, a Trustee who has attended the Conference and voted in favor of a motion may find, upon further consideration, that the needs of D.A. would be seriously undermined if the motion were implemented. Facts later discovered may make a course of conduct appear harmful to the Fellowship. Or, the same Trustee may have voted against the motion and continue to conclude that its implementation would violate a Tradition or Concept of World Service. In such cases, the Trustee would be free to refuse implementation. In that event, the Trustee, and the whole

Board if it agrees with him or her, should be prepared to explain and justify the decision.

This duty to report back to the group is extremely valuable in ensuring that the Right of Decision is exercised appropriately. The person who seeks to invoke this principle should always consider the report that must be rendered and the duty of accountability.

In the end, the Right of Decision provides insurance against the dangers of micromanagement and second-guessing. When an individual has been entrusted with the authority to perform a function, he or she should ordinarily be able to act without fear of unjustified criticism because someone else might have decided differently. While acting within the scope of this authority, one should reasonably expect to be allowed to act as seems fit. Honest decision making should never be condemned, if it is done with care, consideration, and prudence.

Concept Four

❧

Throughout our Conference structure, we maintain at all levels a traditional "Right of Participation," ensuring a voting representation.

One of the fundamental principles in D.A. service is the ideal of equality. To the extent possible in carrying out D.A.'s business, we try to emphasize the basic dignity and inherent worth of every individual. This emphasis on equality underlies both the Fourth and the Fifth Concepts.

As a result, we attempt to ensure that everyone in service—from the groups down to the General Service Board—is accorded the right to participate in the decisional process in a way commensurate with his or her authority and duties. Thus, every group member—and a person is a member if he or she says so—has the right to participate in group business meetings and has a vote equal to that of any other member. If the group has a steering committee, in the steering committee each member of that committee must be consulted and heard whenever possible before a decision is made.

On the Intergroup level, Intergroup Representatives must be consulted at the monthly or quarterly meetings before any major decision is taken or policy change is implemented. This means that meetings must be scheduled at a time and place that is most convenient to the greatest number of representatives, and with sufficient notice to all.

At the World Service Conference, limited time makes it difficult for all who wish to speak to be heard. However, efforts must be made to provide an opportunity for a representative cross-section of the delegates and Trustees present to speak their minds. In D.A. we should be careful not to abuse tactics available in rules of order, such as calling the question, to prevent a full opportunity for all relevant viewpoints to be heard. In all important matters, time rules should be flexible enough to enable the greatest number of GSRs and ISRs to present their arguments. Here it is also important to note that the Office Manager of the General Service Office (GSO) has been given a voice and a vote at the Conference because the experience of that person may be helpful in the decisional process and because that person is the one who will most likely have to answer for Conference decisions.

In meetings of the General Service Board, each member is given an opportunity to speak. Her or his opinion is of equal weight with that of any other Trustee. While the views of an officer may be enlightening in matters affecting that office, and while committee members may have greater expertise on a particular issue relevant to their committee, this special knowledge can never be decisive. All decisions in D.A. should be made only after full participation by all parties.

Finally, the Right of Participation should be viewed as a right of meaningful participation. Each opinion should be accorded the deference and respect that we would want to be given to our own opinions. The fact that a person is perceived as negative or even obstructive should not cause us to close our ears to his or her comments. Even the person we most dislike may be used by the Higher Power to speak the truth if we are willing to listen. We should never be dismissive of any person's contribution to the debate, if we wish to carry out the intent of this Concept.

Concept Five

❧

The traditional Rights of Appeal and Petition protect the minority opinion and ensure the consideration of personal grievances.

Concept Five deals with two related rights: "Appeal" and "Petition." Both are based upon the principle of the equality of all persons involved in service. Even more important, both require courage and a willingness to respect the opinions of a minority. Both involve the recognition that the majority view may be wrong, and that the minority may be articulating the voice of the Higher Power in D.A.'s affairs. Each requires that the majority have the humility to be willing to recognize its own fallibility.

The Right of Appeal refers to the duty of the majority to listen to the minority viewpoint in any debate on issues of importance to D.A. Most frequently, it comes into play after a vote is taken. Whenever there are "no" votes, the Chair should always ask if there is a minority opinion that wishes to be heard. If, as a matter of honestly held principle, a person in the minority believes that the majority has made a serious mistake of principle or fact, that person should rise to restate her or his position for consideration by the majority. Such a power to delay and confuse debate should never be exercised without careful thought. The minority member should never be acting out of hurt feelings or wounded pride, but only out of a deeply held conviction that the decision just reached may seriously harm the D.A. group.

When a member of the minority in D.A. does so, he or she is said to be exercising the Right of Appeal. At that point, the Chair should then ask if anyone who voted with the majority wishes to change her or his mind. If someone is so willing, that person should make a motion to reconsider. If the motion is seconded, a vote will be taken on whether the body wishes to reconsider. If a majority votes to reconsider, then debate on the original question reopens.

This Right of Appeal is of immense spiritual importance. It requires great humility on the part of a majority to recognize that it may have erred. It requires great courage on the part of a member to face down the majority and call it to recognize its duties. And it requires a great degree of respect for the rights of all members to implement this right.

In practice, the Right of Appeal is exercised at the World Service Conference to great effect. At each Conference there will usually be one or two instances in which a member of the minority calls the majority to task for its actions. And, in about half of these cases, the majority will recognize its error and reverse its prior action.

The Right of Petition refers to the right of any personally aggrieved member to seek redress within the service structure. Sometimes this right is misunderstood. It does not mean that a group member has the right to apply to the General Service Board or the Conference to reverse a decision taken by a group. In D.A., the groups are at the top of the inverted service triangle; the General Service Board (GSB) and the World Service Conference (WSC) have no power to discipline or correct a group for its actions. Tradition Four, with its emphasis on group autonomy, states this principle forcefully.

Instead, the right applies to situations in which a member of a group is seeking redress within that body. Thus if the Chair of a business meeting arbitrarily refuses to recognize a member who wishes to speak, that member may turn to the whole group for relief by exercising the Right of Petition. A similar right exists if the Chair of a meeting improperly attempts to exclude or silence a member. When a member believes that a group has acted in violation of the Traditions, she or he has the right to seek to change the group's decision at a later meeting. (In these situations, it should be noted that, while no member may petition the GSB or Conference to reverse a group decision, an aggrieved member may request that the Conference issue a broad statement of policy clarifying the underlying issue for the guidance of all groups in their activities.)

Since the WSC, its committees, the General Service Board, and the General Service Office (GSO) are part of the WSC service framework, the Right of Petition may be exercised within this structure. Thus, if an individual GSR or WSC committee believes that a Trustee or Board committee has acted inappropriately, they may petition the Board for redress of grievances. The Board has adopted a process for resolution of these grievances. Ultimately, if an individual has a grievance against the entire GSB, that person may petition a committee of the Conference to bring a motion to direct the Board to reverse its action. Assuming that there is no infringement of the GSB's legal or fiduciary rights, such a motion would be binding upon the Trustees.

Concept Six

❧

The Conference acknowledges the primary administrative responsibility of the Debtors Anonymous General Service Board.

The Conference and its committees have delegated active management of D.A.'s service activities to the General Service Board (GSB). While many programs that have been proposed are worthwhile, and some have been successful, for purposes of continuity, these programs should be left to the management and supervision of the General Service Board. The GSB has the legal and fiduciary authority to provide a framework under the General Service Office (GSO) to enable these activities to continue, grow, and develop. Where the Board does not have the personnel, time, or money to carry out a particular project, the Conference should recognize that its time has not yet come.

Here, the operative principle is humility. The Conference has recognized, in adopting the Twelve Concepts, that it does not have either the personnel or the expertise to engage in ongoing administrative activities. Whenever it has attempted to do so, difficulties have arisen. The Conference acts through committees, whose memberships change each year. The interests and goals of these members also tend to change and vary. Beyond these practical facts, there lies another spiritual principle. The

Third Step suggests that we turn our will and our lives over to the care of our Higher Power. This tells us that we should not use our wills to beat a recalcitrant reality into submission. If time, personnel, or money for a program is not available, we should accept that fact or, if possible, change it by making the time, money, or personnel available through contributions to the GSO in kind, in cash, or by volunteering. We should not rely on ad hoc, under-supported service structures that are all too likely to collapse in order to impose our viewpoints upon the Fellowship.

It is wise to try to couple policy with administration so that both can be effective. When the Conference, acting as the voice and conscience of the Fellowship, makes a decision, it should always try to couch that decision in terms that are broad and flexible, so that the Board, in administering the decision, can develop policies that are effective. In short, those policy choices that are closely tied to administration are best left with those who are to administer them.

Concept Seven

❧

*The Conference recognizes that the Charter and the Bylaws
of the Debtors Anonymous General Service Board serve as governing
documents and that the Trustees have legal rights, while the rights of the
Conference are spiritual, rooted in the Twelve Traditions.
The Concepts are not legal instruments.*

The Charter of the Debtors Anonymous General Service Board, Inc. is the legal document used to incorporate the D.A. General Service Board (GSB) in the State of New York. It is more commonly called the Articles of Incorporation, and is distinct from the Conference Charter. The general purposes of D.A. as an educational not-for-profit corporation are set forth there. The Bylaws of the Debtors Anonymous General Service Board are more detailed rules covering how our corporate business is conducted under the laws of the State of New York. The bylaws have been adopted by the GSB pursuant to its Articles of Incorporation and are legally binding upon the Board.

These documents stand in contradistinction to the Charter of the D.A. World Service Conference, which has not been filed with any legal entity and does not serve as a legally enforceable document. As a result of its status as a corporation created under the laws of New York State, the General Service Board is the entity legally responsible for carrying out the business affairs of D.A. All property owned by D.A. is legally vested in the Board, and the Board has a fiduciary duty to carry out its responsibilities on behalf of D.A. These are legally binding rights and duties under the laws of New York, and the Board must comply at all times with that jurisdiction's rules, as well as with the rules of any other jurisdiction within which it operates.

Although it does not have any legal significance, the Conference Charter carries great weight within the service structure of D.A. as a whole. It creates and outlines the duties of the World Service Conference (WSC), and sets up the structure whereby the GSB is advised and guided in its actions. Because the Conference represents the collective conscience of all of the D.A. groups in the world, it is apparent that the General Service Office and the Board must ordinarily act with the guidance, support, and general approval of the Conference.

However, as noted in the discussion of Concept Two above, the Board has the right to refuse to follow this guidance in cases where there is an infringement of the legal or fiduciary rights of the Trustees. Thus, the Board has refused to act upon a Conference motion which it concluded was in violation of several Traditions in suggesting that groups might in some cases sell and display outside literature. This right to "veto" WSC actions should be exercised only in the most limited and extreme circumstances. For example, if the Conference directed the Board to enter into a lease beyond the ability of the Fellowship to support it without the possibility of future debting, the Trustees might appropriately refuse to do so. This would be true even if no debting were involved, but the future ability of the Fellowship to carry its message would be impaired.

It is the Conference that carries the spiritual force of the group conscience of D.A., and it is the means by which the heart and soul of the Fellowship—the groups and Intergroups—make certain their will is heard. The Conference is given the power under the GSB Bylaws to ratify the appointment of all Trustees, and as noted in connection with Concept Two, the Conference also holds the ultimate power of the purse, which can be used to control the activities of the Trustees. If the Conference were to decide to withhold group and individual contributions from the GSB and GSO, those entities could no longer exist.

Although the Conference Charter is not a legally binding document, the Board has accepted it as the morally binding expression of the will of the groups as to how D.A.'s business is to be conducted. Under Article 4 of the Conference Charter:

"It will be further understood regardless of the legal prerogatives of the General Service Board, as a matter of tradition, that a three-quarter (3/4) vote of all Conference members present may bring about a reorganization of the General Service Board and staff members of the General Service Office, if or when such reorganization is deemed essential."

Here the Board has accepted the ultimate authority of the Conference in the unlikely situation that the Board has seriously disregarded the moral authority of the Conference. Each Board member is bound by an oath (or affirmation) of office to respect and abide by this provision. In fact, this provision is given legal effect by the voluntary action of the Trustees in adopting Article 3.7 of the Bylaws, which provides in part:

"Class A and Class B Trustees are expected, subject only to the laws of the State of New York and to these Bylaws, at the request of the Conference of Debtors Anonymous, according to the provisions of the D.A. Charter, (that a three-quarter [3/4] vote of all Conference members present may bring about a reorganization of the General Service Board) to resign their trusteeships regardless of whether their term of office has expired."

These carefully limited rights and grants of authority interact to produce a thoughtful balance between power and responsibility. When all is said and done, the ultimate authority of the Conference over the Board, as both a practical and spiritual matter, is apparent, but the Board's legal and fiduciary rights are preserved.

Concept Eight

❧

The Debtors Anonymous General Service Board of Trustees assumes primary leadership for larger matters of overall policy, finance, and custodial oversight, and delegates authority for routine management of the General Service Office.

Concept Eight recognizes, as Concept Six does, that the realities and practicalities of life require that the General Service Board (GSB) take on the role of primary leadership for matters of overall policy. The GSB meets in person and by telephone conference throughout the year. It is a continuing body and has the experience and knowledge necessary to give a broad perspective. The Conference meets for only one short period each year, and its membership changes significantly from year to year—and within the year—as GSR or ISR terms expire and new successors are selected. Although Conference committees meet throughout the year, each has a narrow and limited perspective. For example, the Public Information (PI) Committee focuses solely upon matters relating to public information and cooperation with the professional community. The Hospitals, Institutions and Prisons (HIP) Committee focuses solely upon matters pertaining to these topics. Neither will consider the question of content of literature, which falls to the Literature Committee. What may be desirable for PI may be impossible for HIP. It is the Board which has an overview of all of these activities. The following point should be emphasized here: *No committee is the Conference and no committee can act on behalf of the Conference as a whole without specific and carefully limited authorization.* Only the GSB has been given the right by the Conference Charter to act as a custodian for D.A. as a whole. Any other result would lead to fragmentation.

Moreover, every organization, even those with the least possible structure, like D.A., requires some point at which a final decision can be made and direction can be provided. Any other approach would ultimately result in the demise of the organization. While the Conference can serve as a guide, advisor, and counselor, it cannot serve as a "hands on" director. The Conference may call the GSB to account, and may, on occasion, overrule the GSB, but it cannot engage in active and ongoing operations.

Here the spiritual concept that is in play is that of self-restraint in all things. In exercising its primary leadership role, the GSB must always bear in mind the Second and Ninth Traditions. The Board must accept that is composed of servants, not masters. D.A. does not operate like other corporate entities. We do not have the typical "top down" structure; ordinarily, we do not pass on orders and directives from "the top." Instead, we strive to apply the Steps, Traditions, and Concepts in all of our operations; we attempt to reason and to persuade. Concepts Three, Four, and Five should always influence our thoughts and actions. The Board should accept the fact that its decisions may and should be questioned and challenged. And the Board should always be accountable and be prepared to explain its actions. Most importantly, the Board must always be willing to admit error, if error there be, and strive to correct that error immediately.

Concept Eight also ties directly into Concept Seven. Because the Board has legal rights and duties, it is the only entity in the service structure which can appropriately handle the finances and properties necessary to fulfilling our publishing and other educational functions. Thus, matters of finance and custodial oversight of property are entrusted to the Board. Again, these powers should always be read against the background of the Steps, Traditions, and Concepts. Just like the Conference, the GSB should never become "the seat of perilous wealth or power." The principle of corporate poverty—accumulating only what is necessary to carry out our functions—should be our guide.

Within this context, certain ideas unique to Twelve Step programs are, however, important. Unlike the ordinary employer, the GSB is bound by the Third Concept. We must always strive to avoid micromanagement of the activities of the Office. While the Office is there to assist the Board and D.A. as a whole in carrying out its activities, how it routinely performs these functions should be within the discretion of the staff. This is always subject to the caveat that there may be situations in which the routine itself becomes objectionable and harmful to D.A.'s paramount interests; in such instances, the Trustees have both the right and the obligation to intervene. Decisions should not be imposed upon the Office; under the Fourth Concept, the staff should be consulted before a final decision is made. And, the staff should always be permitted to petition the Board for changes in duties and working conditions under Concept Five.

Concept Nine

෧෨

Good leaders, together with appropriate methods for choosing
them at all levels, are necessary. At the world service level, the Board
of Trustees assumes primary leadership for D.A. as a whole.

Leadership is an important idea for both the Twelve Traditions and the Twelve Concepts. The Second Tradition points out that "our leaders are but trusted servants; they do not govern." This Concept points out the need for good leadership in D.A. But what, precisely, is it?

It is clear that leadership in D.A. is not the same as leadership in the corporate or political worlds. There, leadership takes on an aura of governance. That type of good leader is one who directs or governs well. However, in D.A., the idea of servant leadership is the prevailing approach. This means that the General Service Board (GSB), in exercising its leadership role, must always be aware of the limits of its authority.

First of all, leaders in D.A. must recognize that they exercise only a delegated authority. The right of the Trustees to act on behalf of D.A. stems from the fact that the groups and their delegates have recognized their right to do so. The leaders in D.A. are those who can generate respect and acceptance for their actions because they are understood to be acting for the good of D.A. as a whole. This requires that the Board and

General Service Office (GSO) listen carefully to the D.A. groups as they express themselves in the conscience of the Conference. It is essential that leaders be open to persuasion and discourse. This also applies to group and Intergroup officers and representatives.

This is not to say that good leaders always necessarily follow what they perceive to be the "popular" route. In many instances, the welfare of the whole requires that unpopular actions be taken, and good leaders must be willing to do so when necessary. This leads to a second requirement of good leadership. A leader in D.A. must always be willing to explain her or his actions. Here, clarity and precision are important. Leaders must be sure to think things through and formulate clear and convincing justifications for their contemplated actions. Also, a good leader must be able and willing to lead through persuasion. A calm and reasoned approach will be effective in helping to explain conduct that, at first blush, may be unpopular.

Another element of good leadership is prudence. We must always recognize that our actions in D.A. service have consequences. Those consequences may be serious, whether on the group level or the World Service level. The good leader does not "shoot from the hip" or act on the spur of the moment. Thought and care are important elements of any decision. We should always remember that when we act in service we are acting on behalf of a fellowship that has saved our lives and that will continue to save the lives of others if we act prudently. Rash or impulsive conduct in service is always inappropriate. Just as our personal stories often illustrate that a misplaced sense of urgency can lead to debting, so too can a false urgency result in poor leadership.

Humility is at least as important as prudence. The leaders in a Twelve Step Fellowship must always be willing to recognize and accept their limitations as well as those of others. In service it is all too easy to become self-righteous and insistent upon the need to do things in only one way. This mind frame must be avoided at all costs. The good leader must always be willing to admit error and seek better ways of doing things. Closely allied with this is a sense of humor. The ability to laugh at ourselves is central to good leadership. We must be careful not to take ourselves too seriously, and we must always be ready to place our conduct in the perspective of humor. Beyond this, the ability to laugh and to see the lighter side is helpful in ensuring that we do not become bogged down in our own narrow view of things.

Charity is not only a virtue; it is an essential element of leadership. The ability to reach out and seek to understand and support those around us makes the tasks of all easier. The desire to forgive perceived slights and to move on in unity is of inestimable value. If our service is not motivated by a love of our fellows and a desire to help and assist, it is a vain and empty gesture. Twelfth Step work, at whatever level of service, always proceeds from the impulse of love for our fellows.

Finally, two of the most important elements in leadership are faith and hope. Leaders must have faith in their Higher Power and in the Fellowship of D.A. They must always be willing to strive for the highest good for D.A. Hope leads us on in service to achieve great goals for the Fellowship and for our fellows. Hope convinces us that we can be better and that we can do better.

This sounds like an almost impossible list of attributes for any one person to have. In fact, it may be. Few, if any, among us have all of these qualifications in full measure. But many of us have these attributes to some degree. Some have one or more in great degree. And, when we work together, the full body will have all of these gifts. Our strength is in our unity.

How do we develop and discover these attributes? This is perhaps the hardest question. Sometimes the person possessing these abilities is quiet and these qualities may be obscured by reticence. However, in our groups we come to know each other remarkably well. After all, we have gone through a life-changing experience together in joining D.A. and in working its program. The still, quiet voice often becomes apparent as the voice of wisdom if we listen and continue to love each other. As we grow through working the Twelve Steps, these qualities become increasingly apparent. Experience leads to strength and hope.

Concept Ten

༄

Every D.A. service responsibility should be equal to its service
authority as defined by tradition, resolution, or D.A.'s Charter.

The Tenth Concept states a simple but vital fact: in delegating authority, it is always important to define the scope of that authority clearly and to grant whatever powers may be necessary to carry out this responsibility. This Concept is closely allied with, and flows naturally from, Concept Three. The "Right of Decision" in that Concept provides the means for carrying out the intent of Concept Ten. If we give an individual the responsibility to do something, we must also give that person the necessary authority to accomplish that end. The delegating authority, whether it be the groups, the Conference or the Board, must be careful to relinquish day-to-day control and recognize the right of the recipient of that authority to act as their conscience and knowledge may dictate. It should be noted that this Concept states an ideal. When one is dealing with words, there is almost no way to ensure an absence of ambiguity in both foreseeable and unforeseeable cases. In some cases, ambiguity will develop, no matter how much thought has gone into the words. In such cases, honest efforts must be made to resolve these ambiguities, in light of tradition, the Steps, the Traditions, and other contexts.

Every effort should be made to ensure that the nature and limits of that authority are clearly set forth. Sometimes authority exists from before the time of any grant. Thus, the General Service Board (GSB) pre-existed the writing of the Charter, and much of the Board's authority is defined by tradition that developed in the years before the Conference was created. Here, the Bylaws of the GSB and its Articles of Incorporation (Charter) may contain limitations upon its activities. And again, the Twelve Traditions in D.A. may spell out the limitations on authority. It is clear that all groups are bound by the Fourth Tradition not to engage in conduct that may be harmful to other groups or to D.A. as a whole. It is equally clear that the GSB is bound by the Seventh Tradition's prohibition of outside contributions, and that the Conference is bound by the Tenth Tradition's admonition to avoid "public controversy."

When the Conference creates a new committee, a mission statement is adopted defining the scope of that committee's activities. It is important that no committee exceed its authority or impinge on the duties of any other committee. For example, Conference-approved literature begins with the Literature Committee. While some other committee may request that the Literature Committee consider approving the concept of a particular piece of literature, no other committee should be engaged in writing and/or editing literature.

The GSB delegates authority to run the routine operations of the General Service Office (GSO) to the Office Manager. However, the Board retains a supervisory, policy-making and leadership role in all of the activities of the GSO. At times, it is difficult to define the limits of these two different types of authority. In such cases, there must be an effort made to ensure that there is no overreaching. Where there is doubt, efforts must be made to seek clarity. It is obvious, however, that the Board must remain the final authority with respect to actions taken, since it is legally responsible for all GSO activities.

Concept Eleven

❧

While the Trustees hold final authority for D.A. World Service administration, they will be assisted by the best possible staff members and consultants. Therefore, serious care and consideration will always be given to the compensation, selection, induction to service, rotation, and assignments for special rights and duties for all staff with a proper basis for determining financial compensation.

The status, selection, and pay of staff and consultants are the subjects of this Concept. Most important is the injunction that the General Service Board (GSB) exercise serious care and consideration in using its authority in this area.

As a small fellowship, D.A. does not have a large staff. At this writing, there is one full-time Office Manager and one part-time staff assistant. In the past, care has been taken in selecting the Manager, and their selection of an assistant has been done in consultation with the GSB. This procedure should continue; if another full-time employee is hired, it is to be expected that the Board would have similar input into his or her selection. While matters of general policy remain with the Trustees, the means by which these policies and goals are attained have been left to the initial discretion of the Manager, subject to general policy. The Board oversees the Office and its employees through an Office Committee, which includes an Office Liaison who regularly communicates with the Office Manager. An annual review of the work of the Office Manager is undertaken by the Office Liaison, and this is reported to the Office Committee and the full Board.

The Board gives great attention to the matter of compensation. Again, as a small fellowship, we must pay close attention to finances. However, this does not mean that we are miserly. The Trustees have an obligation to hire the best possible staff, and this means that our wages must be competitive to ensure that we hire and retain experienced and capable employees. Each year the Office Committee of the Board undertakes a review of the full-time salary of the Office Manager as well as the benefits that are provided. The Office Committee, in conjunction with the Finance Committee, takes great care and deliberation in this area, and the full Board reviews and approves any final decision as to compensation.

This Concept also deals with the relation of the General Service Board to the General Service Office. Here, the principle of "custodial oversight" must be balanced against the idea of delegation of "routine management." From the start, it should be clear that the relation between the GSB and the staff of the GSO is, ultimately, the relation of employer to employee. Employee professionalism and dedication are underlying principles of that relationship, just like respect, fairness, and honesty on the part of the Board. The World Service Conference is not a direct participant in this relationship. That authority has been delegated by the groups to the Trustees. Without a clear understanding of this principle, we would be entering the dangerous fields of double-headed management. While the Conference or a committee may advise, it should never interfere.

The Board has employed outside consultants most often in the areas of legal and technology/Internet services. We also employ outside assistance in the editorial preparation, layout, translation, and publication of our literature and some reports. We have sometimes been fortunate in finding members of the Board who have been generous with their services in these areas, providing free assistance. When outsiders are chosen, efforts are made to ensure that their rates are competitive and that they will perform competently. In small matters, the Board will dispense with competitive bids, particularly where speed is of the essence, but in any large-scale employment, such as the contract for writing the Twelve Steps and Twelve Traditions book, requests for proposals are used. In all non-bidding situations, the committee supervising the activity usually has a clear understanding of what rates are competitive.

This Concept on its face applies only to staff and consultants hired by the Trustees. However, it provides a model for the groups and Intergroups as well, in selecting their officers and committees. Thus, great care should be exercised in the selection of a treasurer. Prudent supervision of our finances must always be our goal in Debtors Anonymous. Experience and recovery are important qualifications in this area. The position of GSR or ISR should also be given careful consideration. When a person is selected to fill one of those positions, she or he will be making decisions that may affect the future of D.A. for years to come. We should give at least as much care to the selection of such people as we would give to the selection of those who are to care for our children. After all, D.A. is the future of all of us.

Concept Twelve

❧

*The Conference of Debtors Anonymous will observe the spirit of the
Traditions, taking care not to become powerful and wealthy;
having sufficient operating funds with a prudent reserve; having no
authority over any other members; making important decisions by
discussing and voting on issues wherever possible by substantial unanimity;
not acting in a punitive way; not inciting public controversy;
never performing any acts of government; and finally, always
remaining democratic in thought and action.*

Concept Twelve contains what are called the "General Warranties" of the Conference. Similar language is contained in Article 10 of the Conference Charter, and may be changed only with the consent of three-quarters of the registered groups in D.A. Since this is the same requirement for amending the Twelve Steps and the Twelve Traditions, it is obvious how important these Warranties were to those who founded the Fellowship of Debtors Anonymous.

Each of these Warranties is related to fundamental ideas in our spiritual program of recovery.

Concept Twelve

"taking care not to become powerful and wealthy"

Here, the Second and Seventh Traditions are best recalled. We are reminded again of the humbling fact that our leaders are only trusted servants. They do not govern. They have no power to discipline or expel. Instead, they operate on the basis of their honest understanding of what the will of the Higher Power is for D.A., putting aside personal goals, ambitions, and resentments. Just as the General Service Board (GSB) is bound by the ideal of corporate poverty, so is the Conference.

"having sufficient operating funds with a prudent reserve"

The Second Warranty is one that goes to the heart of the D.A. recovery program. Careful supervision of our finances is a duty of the Conference, just as it is an individual responsibility for all members as well as the Trustees of the General Service Board. We are to put into practice on the service level what we have learned on the recovery level.

"having no authority over any other members"

The Third Warranty stands in stark contrast to corporate or political models of social organization. The Conference has no power to direct the recovery of any individual. While it may put forward suggestions and share with the Board the experience, strength, and hope of D.A. members over the decades, it may not mandate a course of conduct, either in recovery or in other parts of our lives. How each member achieves his or her spiritual life is a matter of individual conscience. The Conference, unlike a church or other spiritual body, has no right to attempt to direct that conscience.

"making important decisions by discussing and voting on issues wherever possible by substantial unanimity"

The Fourth Warranty's requirements of discussion and substantial unanimity ensure that D.A.'s Conference will act thoughtfully and prudently. This ties in with the Rights of Appeal and Petition of the Fifth Concept. The Conference must always make an effort to listen to and consider the minority voice. Deliberations should not be hasty; we should always be willing to reconsider in matters of importance. When actions are taken, they should reflect the clear will of the membership; a mere majority should not be able to impose its will on a substantial minority. Thus, a two-thirds vote has, in practice, been required for most major decisions of the Conference.

"not acting in a punitive way"

The requirement of Warranty Five reinforces the idea that the Conference does not exercise authority over the membership of D.A. There is no enforcement mechanism in D.A. to allow the Conference to impose its will upon members. There is no right of censure or expulsion[7], no excommunication or denial of membership. The Conference reflects the voice and the conscience of D.A. as a whole. That is the source of whatever authority it might have in a moral sense. It has none in a worldly sense. Like all of the other Warranties, this should also apply at the group and Intergroup levels. There should be no room for punishment in D.A. Love and service should be our motto.

---

7. Keeping in mind, however, the example given previously in Concept Three; i.e., the group Chair, in order to preserve group unity (per Tradition One), has both the duty and right to prevent an individual from disrupting an ongoing meeting.

"not inciting public controversy"

The Sixth Warranty is closely related to the Tenth Tradition. As a group, D.A. has no opinion on outside issues; we should always refrain from conduct that might appear to be an endorsement or support of anything outside our primary purpose. This does not mean that the Conference should not debate issues that properly come before it. Disagreement is the anvil on which truth is forged. We must always be willing to assert our honestly held opinions when this will further the good of D.A.; it is never appropriate to involve D.A. in controversy on outside issues.

"never performing any acts of government"

Under the Seventh Warranty, the Conference, including the General Service Board, should never perform acts of government. It should not seek to bind the membership to any belief system or code of conduct. It should recognize the importance of the individual in D.A. And it should accept that differences in approach and opinion will always exist in a free society.

"always remaining democratic in thought and action."

Finally, the Eighth Warranty is a guarantee that D.A. will always adhere to democratic principles in conducting its business. If we adhere to the other Concepts, the Steps, and the Traditions, this should pose no problem. Throughout its history, D.A. has emphasized the right of individual conscience and the rights of individuals. Democracy implies this and more. It implies a corresponding duty on the part of the minority to accept the majority decision as the will of the Higher Power. There should be no efforts to undermine, or walking away in anger. If a mistake has been made, it will eventually become apparent to most. At that time, and only then, should efforts be made to change the decision of the majority reached by substantial unanimity.

❧

The Twelve Concepts for Debtors Anonymous were inspired by the Twelve Concepts for Alcoholics Anonymous and are modified with permission of A.A. World Services, Inc.

Made in United States
North Haven, CT
30 June 2023

38406900R00089